Data Analysis and Business Modeling with Excel 2013

Manage, analyze, and visualize data with Microsoft Excel 2013 to transform raw data into ready-to-use information

David Rojas

[PACKT] PUBLISHING enterprise
professional expertise distilled

BIRMINGHAM - MUMBAI

Data Analysis and Business Modeling with Excel 2013

First published: October 2015

Production reference: 1191015

Published by Packt Publishing Ltd.
Livery Place
35 Livery Street
Birmingham B3 2PB, UK.

ISBN 978-1-78528-954-5

www.packtpub.com

Credits

Author
David Rojas

Reviewers
Skanda Bhargav
Manoj Kumar
Rajesh S
Kimberly J. E. Williamson

Commissioning Editor
Veena Pagare

Acquisition Editor
Sonali Vernekar

Content Development Editor
Parita Khedekar

Technical Editor
Madhunikita Sunil Chindarkar

Copy Editor
Rashmi Sawant

Project Coordinator
Milton Dsouza

Proofreader
Safis Editing

Indexer
Hemangini Bari

Production Coordinator
Shantanu N. Zagade

Cover Work
Shantanu N. Zagade

About the Author

David Rojas is a data enthusiast and Python evangelist. Currently, he is enjoying his time as a consultant in the data world. He lives in the Silicon Valley and is active within the data community. After receiving a degree from the University of Florida as an industrial and systems engineer and obtaining a minor in sales engineering, he received his state license as an engineer in training. Soon thereafter, he pursued a career change to the IT world as a data analyst and discovered his passion for data using various tools in order to manage and analyze data in a better way. After many years of working in a wide range of odd data roles, such as reporting, gathering requirements, writing documentation, working with databases, and working with flat files, he decided to make his love for data a reality and started his own business (www.hedaro.com). You will often find his work being cited by various professors and other data enthusiasts around the Bay Area.

About the Reviewers

Skanda Bhargav is an engineering graduate from Visvesvaraya Technological University (VTU) in Belgaum, Karnataka, India. He did his major in computer science engineering. He is a Cloudera-certified developer in Apache Hadoop. His interests are big data and Hadoop.

He is the author of the book *Troubleshooting Ubuntu Server*, *Packt Publishing*. He has been a reviewer for the following books and videos:

- Building Hadoop Clusters
- Hadoop Cluster Deployment
- Instant Map Reduce Patterns – Hadoop Essentials How-to [Instant]
- Cloudera Administration Handbook
- Hadoop Map Reduce v2 Cookbook – Second Edition
- Hadoop Backup and Recovery Solutions

I would like to thank my family for their immense support and faith in me throughout my learning stage. My friends have brought the confidence in me to a level that makes me bring the best out of myself. I am happy that god has blessed me with such wonderful people around me, without whom, my success as it is today would not have been possible.

Manoj Kumar holds a degree of bachelor of technology in mining and machinery engineering from the Indian School of Mines, an executive MBA degree in finance and operations from ICFAI and is certified in data science from the Johns Hopkins University. He has over 13 years of work experience in mining, cement, and other industries in multiple countries. Currently, he is working as a subject matter expert and data scientist for Cyient Insights, a data science division of Cyient Ltd. He uses part of data science to perform statistical analysis on domain-specific data (such as sensor and other high frequency, structured and unstructured both, and so on). In order to arrive at conclusions that add value to the business and help in decision making, he focuses on the development and application of high-end mathematical modeling/algorithm of big data, generated by industries (for example, mining and manufacturing).

Rajesh S is a management professional and graduate in computer science. He has over a decade of experience in retail MNCs. His skills include data analysis and its presentation.

He has a website that helps, guides, and enriches a lot of professionals who vouch for his excellent coaching through his "Excelhours", a personal coaching program (Microsoft Excel).

I am grateful to the almighty god for his grace and mercy that has bought me this far and made me the person I am today. I would like to thank my wife Jyoti, who has helped and supported me throughout all my ups and downs in life.

Kimberly J. E. Williamson is a home-grown data analyst with experience in financial and budget analysis, business tax management, commercial lease analysis, and administration, among other areas. Having built a reputation for proactively learning whatever is needed to excel in her business or personal projects, she loves diving into data and wrangling it into an intelligent form as well as creating best practice processes for the creation, management, and usability of data.

Kimberly often self-contracts financial or data analysis work through her own company, Strategic Resource Development, LLC, and financially manages this company as well as her husband's company, Sophos, LLC, which owns rental properties. She has worked in a diverse array of environments, such as nonprofit, medical property management, the private loan market, banking, engineering, project management, and so on.

Although this is the first time she has been formally asked to provide a technical review, in the past she has contributed heavily to the creation and editing of complex in-house accounting and data management procedural guides for commercial lease management.

I'd like to thank both Jesus Christ and Packt Publishing for giving me the opportunity to explore this new avenue to use my skills (and learn some new ones) as a technical reviewer of this book.

www.PacktPub.com

Support files, eBooks, discount offers, and more

For support files and downloads related to your book, please visit www.PacktPub.com.

Did you know that Packt offers eBook versions of every book published, with PDF and ePub files available? You can upgrade to the eBook version at www.PacktPub.com and as a print book customer, you are entitled to a discount on the eBook copy. Get in touch with us at service@packtpub.com for more details.

At www.PacktPub.com, you can also read a collection of free technical articles, sign up for a range of free newsletters and receive exclusive discounts and offers on Packt books and eBooks.

https://www2.packtpub.com/books/subscription/packtlib

Do you need instant solutions to your IT questions? PacktLib is Packt's online digital book library. Here, you can search, access, and read Packt's entire library of books.

Why subscribe?

- Fully searchable across every book published by Packt
- Copy and paste, print, and bookmark content
- On demand and accessible via a web browser

Free access for Packt account holders

If you have an account with Packt at www.PacktPub.com, you can use this to access PacktLib today and view 9 entirely free books. Simply use your login credentials for immediate access.

Instant updates on new Packt books

Get notified! Find out when new books are published by following @PacktEnterprise on Twitter or the *Packt Enterprise* Facebook page.

Table of Contents

Preface

If you ever wondered how other data professionals manage, analyze, and visualize data with Excel, then this book will be a wealth of knowledge for you. This book is filled with step-by-step instructions and progresses through the same natural stages a data analyst goes through in practice. The examples are deliberately small so that you can understand the problems being solved and solutions are shown in detail without skipping any steps along the way. In addition, my extensive experience in the industry will help you explore practical real-world examples that go beyond theories and provide you with a strong foundation that can be used in a wide range of data-intensive roles that you may encounter throughout your career. After reading the entire book, you will have the confidence to work with data and tell a compelling story about its findings using Excel.

What this book covers

Chapter 1, *Getting Data into Excel*, covers several examples of how you can create your own data or bring data into Excel from various sources. Data can come from many sources, and in practice, you will normally find data in flat files, such as CSV or Excel.

Chapter 2, *Connecting to Databases*, covers how to connect to a Microsoft SQL Server database, although there are various flavors of databases. Step-by-step examples are provided to give you plenty of practice. Nearly, all of the organizations that you will analyze data for will store all of the data in a relational database.

Chapter 3, *How to Clean Texts, Numbers, and Dates*, covers how to clean data or prepare data for analysis, which is one of the most time-consuming steps in the data analysis life cycle. Cleaning data is a must-have skill for anyone working with data. *Bad* data can come from various sources, such as manually entered data, bad web forms that allow erroneous data to enter a company's database, or bugs in software, which can all lead to very messy data that you have to deal with. In this chapter, we will also take a look at several examples of how to deal with strings, numbers, and dates in Excel.

Chapter 4, *Using Formulas to Prepare Your Data for Analysis*, covers the use of Excel's formulas to create custom columns, identify key metrics, and make decisions based on business rules. Formulas are one of the key features that showcase the power of the tool, and this chapter provides you with plenty of practical examples to help you gain valuable experience.

Chapter 5, *Analyzing Your Data Using Descriptive Statistics and Charts*, uses Excel to explore data to identify bad data, spot outliers, and trends. After data has been cleaned and prepared, it is now time to dig a little deeper. Are there any issues with your data? Do you have bad data? Do you understand what kind of data is in each column and how it relates to the rest of your dataset? Using Excel's built-in tools and charting capabilities, you will learn more about the data you are working with.

Chapter 6, *Link Your Data Using Data Models*, covers how to combine and link data using database concepts by taking advantage of the new features of Excel 2013. Excel's data model allowa us to combine tables in a similar way to how the LOOKUP functions accomplished this previously. This new functionality will allow the analyst to merge datasets faster and with ease. Organizing data is the key concept in this chapter that will propel you to answer questions about the data.

Chapter 7, *A Primer on Using the Excel Solver*, teaches you the basics of the Excel Solver, which is one of the most underrated tools that comes with Excel. You will learn how to activate the add-ins all the way through to solving business problems that are relevant to today's workplace. The information in these few pages will elevate you above other Excel developers.

Chapter 8, *Learning VBA – Excel's Scripting Language*, introduces you to Excel's very own scripting language. After performing the same data transformations over and over again, a smart data analyst will try to find ways to automate repetitive tasks. Excel's solution to this problem is VBA (Visual Basic for Applications), in which you will learn how to create macros to automate certain tasks. This chapter will empower you with knowledge that will differentiate you from a casual Excel user to a powerful, skilled, and advanced Excel developer.

Chapter 9, *How to Build and Style Your Charts*, discusses how to use Excel's built-in charting tools to quickly create visually appealing charts. Visualizing data is not only a great way to understand it but also a great way to tell a story to an audience. This chapter also covers how to customize properties, such as titles, legends, colors, and so on. This chapter focuses on the keys to generate creative, simple, and concise charts that will deliver insights from your findings.

Chapter 10, Creating Interactive Spreadsheets Using Tables and Slicers, helps you leverage Excel's interactive slicers, which is one of the most exciting chapters in this book that will simply impress you. Here, you will gain the ability to slice and dice data interactively, create custom filters that automatically update the data on the fly, and watch the audience engage with the data. You can filter by dates, strings, and numbers; the possibilities are endless!

Appendix, Tips, Tricks, and Shortcuts, provides you with useful shortcuts and tips that have been used throughout this book for reference purposes.

What you need for this book

You will need a copy of the Microsoft Office Home and Student 2013 software. In addition, you will also need an up-to-date Windows laptop or desktop.

Who this book is for

This book is for new and experienced Excel users who want to enhance their skills in the data analysis life cycle. This includes gathering, preparing, modeling, and finally, presenting data. This book also has everything a data analyst would ever want to know, including how to clean data retrieved from databases, use advanced Excel tools, and create interactive spreadsheets.

Conventions

In this book, you will find a number of text styles that distinguish between different kinds of information. Here are some examples of these styles and an explanation of their meaning.

Code words in text, database table names, folder names, filenames, file extensions, pathnames, dummy URLs, user input, and Twitter handles are shown as follows: "But for your reference, Excel looks for HTML `<table>` tags to identify tables on a website."

A block of code is set as follows:

```
SELECT *
FROM pmthistory a
JOIN users b on (a.userid = b.id)
```

New terms and **important words** are shown in bold. Words that you see on the screen, for example, in menus or dialog boxes, appear in the text like this: "If we did not have the **Clear All Filters** button, the users would have to figure out how they would clear every slicer one at a time to start over."

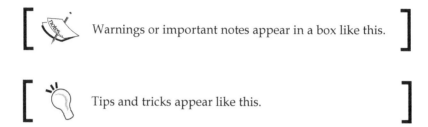

Warnings or important notes appear in a box like this.

Tips and tricks appear like this.

Reader feedback

Feedback from our readers is always welcome. Let us know what you think about this book—what you liked or disliked. Reader feedback is important for us as it helps us develop titles that you will really get the most out of.

To send us general feedback, simply e-mail feedback@packtpub.com, and mention the book's title in the subject of your message.

If there is a topic that you have expertise in and you are interested in either writing or contributing to a book, see our author guide at www.packtpub.com/authors.

Customer support

Now that you are the proud owner of a Packt book, we have a number of things to help you to get the most from your purchase.

Downloading the example code

You can download the example code files from your account at http://www.packtpub.com for all the Packt Publishing books you have purchased. If you purchased this book elsewhere, you can visit http://www.packtpub.com/support and register to have the files e-mailed directly to you.

Downloading the color images of this book

We also provide you with a PDF file that has color images of the screenshots/diagrams used in this book. The color images will help you better understand the changes in the output. You can download this file from `https://www.packtpub.com/sites/default/files/downloads/9545EN_ColorImages.pdf`.

Errata

Although we have taken every care to ensure the accuracy of our content, mistakes do happen. If you find a mistake in one of our books—maybe a mistake in the text or the code—we would be grateful if you could report this to us. By doing so, you can save other readers from frustration and help us improve subsequent versions of this book. If you find any errata, please report them by visiting `http://www.packtpub.com/submit-errata`, selecting your book, clicking on the **Errata Submission Form** link, and entering the details of your errata. Once your errata are verified, your submission will be accepted and the errata will be uploaded to our website or added to any list of existing errata under the Errata section of that title.

To view the previously submitted errata, go to `https://www.packtpub.com/books/content/support` and enter the name of the book in the search field. The required information will appear under the **Errata** section.

Piracy

Piracy of copyrighted material on the Internet is an ongoing problem across all media. At Packt, we take the protection of our copyright and licenses very seriously. If you come across any illegal copies of our works in any form on the Internet, please provide us with the location address or website name immediately so that we can pursue a remedy.

Please contact us at `copyright@packtpub.com` with a link to the suspected pirated material.

We appreciate your help in protecting our authors and our ability to bring you valuable content.

Questions

If you have a problem with any aspect of this book, you can contact us at `questions@packtpub.com`, and we will do our best to address the problem.

1
Getting Data into Excel

Thank you for taking the first step to becoming a knowledgeable and experienced Excel developer. You will learn how to manually create data in Excel and how to import data from various flat files, such as text, CSV, and Excel. By the end of this chapter, we will learn how to consume data from the Web.

Getting started with data

Before we get started with Excel, let's go through the **data analysis life cycle**. These are the steps that should be taken every time you perform some sort of data analysis. The steps include gathering, preparing, analyzing, and presenting data. While you may not always be responsible for every step in the data analysis life cycle, every step is dependent on each other. Enough talking, let's take a moment to define each step.

Gathering data

Gathering data is exactly what it sounds like; in this step, you will be gathering all of the data you need for analysis. This might include data that you get from your client, boss, coworker, the Internet, or a database. There are other data sources, such as CSV files, but remember that it is your job to find the data. I once had a client asking me "Can you take a look at my code as it is not working?" He was trying to map some data into Google Maps and he was having trouble doing this. He sent me code snippets and asked me if I could figure out what the problem was. I took a look at his work, but I just did not have enough information to debug the issue. Guess what my next question to my client was? "Send me your code and the *data* you are trying to plot." Knowing what kind of data my client was working with and what the code was doing with the data were the two key questions that I needed to know.

I eventually figured out the issue for my client, but the point here is to show you that getting the data in your hands is the first step. *Chapter 1, Getting Data into Excel,* and *Chapter 2, Connecting to Databases,* will focus on providing you with all the skills needed to bring data from various sources into Excel.

Preparing data

You will soon realize that after you gather your data, it does not always come in a neat package for you. For example, you may be given a PDF document with 1,000 entries and asked to transfer that data into an Excel spreadsheet. You might get lucky and be able to copy/paste the records into Excel, or you might be forced to manually enter each record by hand. I used to work for a wholesaler of college text books and faced a similar situation. I needed to copy a very large PDF document and transfer its content to Excel. I remember refusing to do so and asking a coworker to put this data in a different format. I was trying everything under my control to avoid that PDF file. Unfortunately, in the end I had no choice but to roll up my sleeves and get the job done. As a data analyst, you would probably spend most of your time in the data analysis life cycle *cleaning* the data. In other words, you will gather data and organize it in a format you can work with. Munging and data wrangling are other terms you may hear that refer to this step of the process. Other common issues are numbers formatted as strings, missing values, extra spaces, and so on. We will go through various examples of the ones mentioned and their solutions in *Chapter 3, How to Clean Texts, Numbers, and Dates,* and *Chapter 4, Using Formulas to Prepare Your Data for Analysis.*

Analyzing data

After you gather and prepare your data, you are now ready to analyze it. Your main goal up until now was to get your data into Excel; this is our comfort zone where we know we can work with data. What do I mean when I say analyze your data? Well, this means that it is time to get your inquisitive and curious hats on. If you don't have any of these, then it is time to act like a detective, Inspector Gadget style (if you're old enough to remember who he is). In this step, we begin with inspecting every column one by one. For example, let's say that the first column was called **Revenue** and the second column was called **Product Name**. We would expect the **Revenue** column to have numbers in each of the values and the **Product Name** column to have strings as the values associated with this column. We will then look for any missing values, the largest number, and the smallest value. We might also take a look at the distinct values in the **Product Name** column and look for any misspelled words.

Are you trying to solve a problem? Are you trying to predict the next year's revenue? Did you ask for some background of the task you were assigned to do? Remember to ask all these questions to whoever is going to receive your analysis for feedback along the way. The last thing that you might avoid is that when you complete the analysis, you are told that you were analyzing or solving the wrong problem. You may also spend a lot of time figuring out what certain columns mean if you actually have the data to complete the task. *Chapter 5*, *Analyzing Your Data Using Descriptive Statistics and Charts*, *Chapter 6*, *Link Your Data Using Data Models*, and *Chapter 7*, *A Primer on Using the Excel Solver*, will give you enough exposure to analyzing and squeezing out insights from your data.

Presenting data

This is where the fun begins; you are now at a point where you can tell your story. At this point, you should know everything about your data, such as where it came from and how it was prepared or organized, and you should have completed the task you were assigned, at least in theory. For example, if you were asked to simply create a line chart with the monthly sales for the year, then this is where you should be at this stage. The data should be in Excel, the sales data should be aggregated on a monthly basis, and you should already have an idea of how to create and place your line chart. Before you spend an hour or so making your final spreadsheet look good, create a simple mockup and get feedback from your end user. I know that this is not always applicable to every situation, but getting feedback along the way will save you a lot of time from redoing the work at a later stage. Another little known fact is that people just change their minds or sometimes change their requirements, so always build your spreadsheets as flexible as possible. In our example, you may be asked to switch the data from *quarterly* to *monthly* for an analysis at the last minute. They may want the data over the past 5 years and a bar chart instead of a line chart. My advice to you is very simple; expect changes every single time. Luckily, Excel has many wonderful tools to help you spin up interactive and visually impressive workbooks. In *Chapter 9*, *How to Build and Style Your Charts*, and *Chapter 10*, *Creating Interactive Spreadsheets Using Tables and Slicers*, we will go through all these neat features that will equip you with the necessary knowledge to further enhance your skills.

Manually creating data

Let's create our first dataset by using the following steps:

1. First, fire up Excel 2013 and create a new spreadsheet. We will begin with creating some data manually as an introduction to gathering data. We will begin with typing in cell **A1**, as shown in the following screenshot:

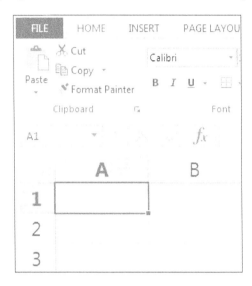

2. Type Revenue in cell **A1** and Name in cell **B1**, as shown in the following screenshot. These are going to be our column headings of our dataset.

3. We are now going to apply styles to the column headings so that they stand out. Highlight columns **A1** and **B1** and press *Ctrl + B*. This action will make the two strings that we selected *bold*. Another option is to highlight the cells and click on the **Bold** button in the toolbar, as shown in the following screenshot:

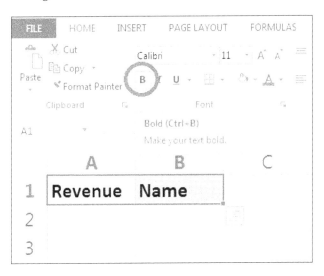

4. Now, type 321, 45, 7, and 23 in the **Revenue** column. Then, type David, Bob, Bill, and Mike in the **Name** column. Your spreadsheet should look like the example in the following screenshot:

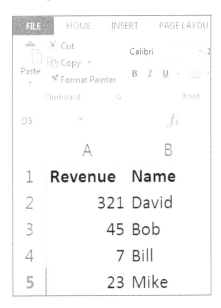

5. For our finishing touches, we can apply styles to our data by adding borders around the cells. We can accomplish this by highlighting the cells **A1** through **B5** and clicking on the **Borders** button. This will bring up a new menu. Select **All Borders**. Remember that you need to first highlight the cells you want to add the borders to. Refer to the following screenshot:

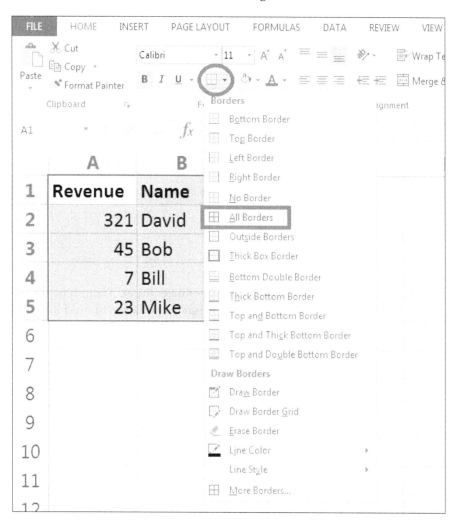

Congratulations! You have just learned how to enter numbers, strings, and column headers in an Excel spreadsheet. You have also learned how to apply styles to the text and cells using various built-in Excel functions. You can think of this as your first *Hello World* program in Excel 2013. Your final output should look like this:

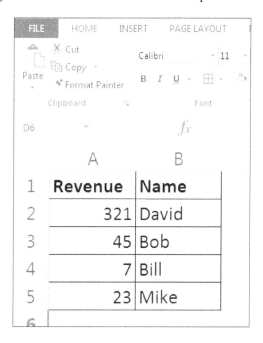

Importing data from various sources

In this section, we are going to cover the sources the data is imported from. They are as follows:

- Importing data from a text file
- Importing a CSV file
- Importing other Excel files
- Importing data from the Web

Importing data from a text file

There are times when data comes in a text file, and to be honest, this can be a scary thing. I am saying this because data that comes in a text file can be formatted in many ways, and you never know what you are going to get. Luckily, most of the time you will get comma-separated data and this is something Excel can consume pretty easily. Let's start with creating our own text file and then importing it into Excel:

1. Open Notepad or a similar text editor. Copy and paste the following chunk of data into the text file, as shown in the following screenshot:

   ```
   Revenue,Name
   321,David
   45,Bob
   7,Bill
   23,Mike
   ```

   Then, save the file as `data.txt` on your desktop.

2. Now, open Excel and create a new workbook. Go to the **DATA** tab and click on the **From Text** button, as shown in the following screenshot:

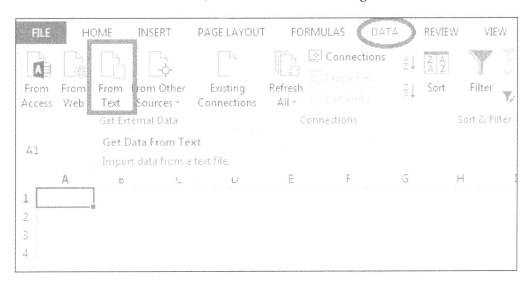

Navigate to your data.txt file and click on the **Import** button, as shown in the following screenshot:

3. You will now see a dialog box, as shown in the following screenshot. This dialog box will ask you how your data has been formatted. By default, you will have the **Delimited** option selected. This means that your data is separated by some characters such as spaces, commas, and semicolons. In our example, the values in the data.txt file are separated by commas. There are other options, but 99 percent of the time, you can just click on the **Next** button.

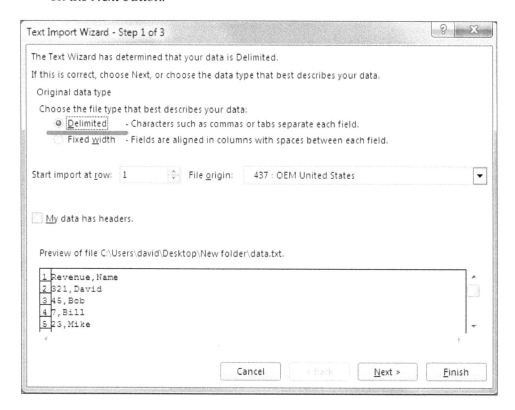

4. Step two of the import wizard will now ask you to select the delimiter or the character that separates each of the values you are trying to import. Make sure that you click on the **Comma** delimiter and remove any other options that may have been checked automatically.

Now, let's take a look at the **Data preview** area in the following screenshot. This area will show you a few records of how Excel plans to parse the data. As shown in the following screenshot, we can see that by choosing the **Comma** delimiter, Excel correctly splits the data into two columns. We can now click on the **Finish** button.

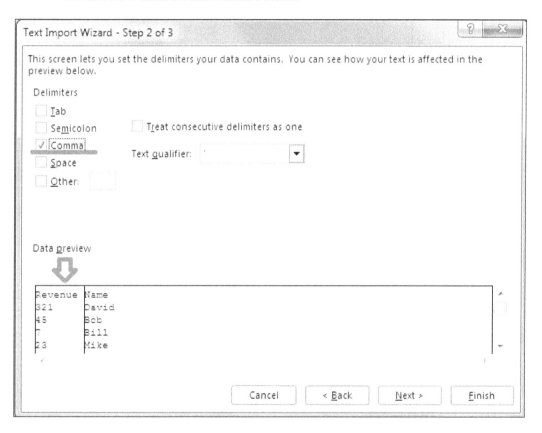

5. The last dialog box will ask you to select where you want to paste the data. The default value is **A1** and this is usually the cell you would like to insert the data into. At this point, you also have the option to paste your data into a new worksheet by choosing this option in the dialog box.

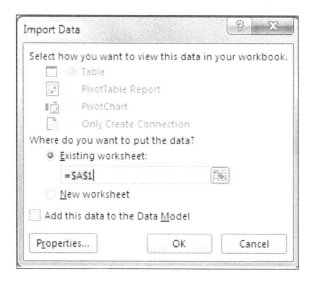

After you click on the **OK** button, you will see your data in columns **A** and **B**.

You can also drag the actual `data.txt` file into Excel and this will activate the **Text Import Wizard**.

Importing a CSV file

The acronym CSV means comma-separated values. What this means to us is that when we use the **Text Import Wizard**, we need to select **Comma** as the delimiter. To import a CSV file, the steps are exactly the same as those in the *Manually creating data* section; however, the `data.txt` file is not a CSV file. A CSV file can be identified by its filename ending in `.csv`.

Importing other Excel files

If you perform the same steps that we just learned to import a text or a CSV file into an Excel workbook, then all that Excel does is open the file you are trying to import. It will not ask you for a delimiter, it will not open the **Text Import Wizard**, and it will simply open the Excel file. Let's go through a simple example to show you how to correctly merge multiple Excel files:

1. Make two separate Excel files using the same techniques, as shown in the *Manually creating data* section. Split the dataset that we have been using, create one spreadsheet with the **Revenue** column, and create a second spreadsheet with the **Name** column.

    File one should be called one.xlsx and the file will look like this:

    File two should be called two.xlsx and will look similar to the following screenshot:

	A	B
1	Name	
2	David	
3	Bob	
4	Bill	
5	Mike	

Now, let's pause and see what we are trying to do here with the two files. The goal is to combine them into one file. There are two methods that we can use, so let's start with the easiest one.

In the first method, open the `one.xlsx` and `two.xlsx` files. Using the `two.xlsx` file, highlight columns **A1** through **A5**. Press *Ctrl + C* to copy the selected cells. Now, switch to the `one.xlsx` file and select column **B1**. Press *Ctrl + V* to paste the data. Your spreadsheet should now look like the following screenshot:

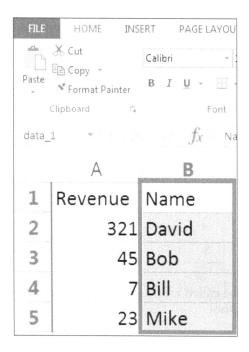

Congratulations! At this point, you can save the file as `final.xlsx` and you are all done. You have combined two different Excel workbooks into one.

The second method involves using an Excel feature that you will often use in different situations. Let's go through the following steps, and then, I will explain the benefits of using this technique:

1. Open the `one.xlsx` and `two.xlsx` files. Using the `one.xlsx` file, right-click on the tab named **Sheet 1**, and select the **Move or Copy...** option, as shown here:

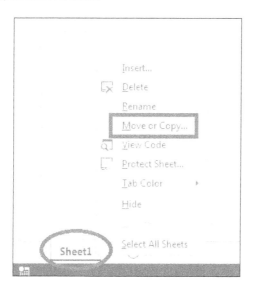

The **Move or Copy** dialog box will appear. Select the workbook that you plan to move the data to. In this case, it is going to be `01 - Chapter - two.xls`. Make sure that you have the second workbook open, or you will not be able to see this option in the drop-down menu. In the next section named **Before sheet**, select the option called **(move to end)**, check the **Create a copy** checkbox, and click on the **OK** button, as shown here:

You will now have your second spreadsheet with two tabs: one named **Sheet 1** that holds your original data and another one named **Sheet 1 (2)** that holds the data we just imported from the first spreadsheet. From here on, we can just employ the first technique and combine both the datasets. Good job!

What was so different about the second method? This method gives us options and that is the key. We currently have a spreadsheet that contains the raw data from each of the two workbooks. We can then create a third spreadsheet or a third tab that holds the data from the two datasets. If we make any mistakes, we can simply remake the third tab/spreadsheet, as our original data is still intact. We can also filter the data of our two original datasets before we combine any data. In practice, you will notice that you will be performing a unique combination of these two methods, depending on your dataset and the problem you are trying to solve.

Importing data from the Web

Here, we will learn how to grab data from the Web. This is the least common task that you will be asked to perform from the previous lessons but taking a look at how it is done is worth your time. We will go through a typical scenario in the following steps:

1. Open Excel 2013 and create a new spreadsheet. The next steps will involve opening a web page in Excel and extracting data from a table found on the website. We will start with selecting the **DATA** tab and clicking on the **From Web** button, as shown in the following screenshot:

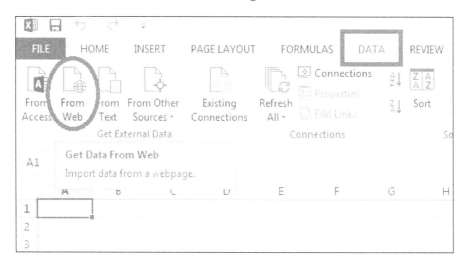

2. A dialog box will appear. In the **Address** textbox, type
`http://pandasbootcamp.herokuapp.com` and click on the **Go** button. After
the page has been loaded, you will see a similar **new web query** dialog box,
as shown in the following screenshot:

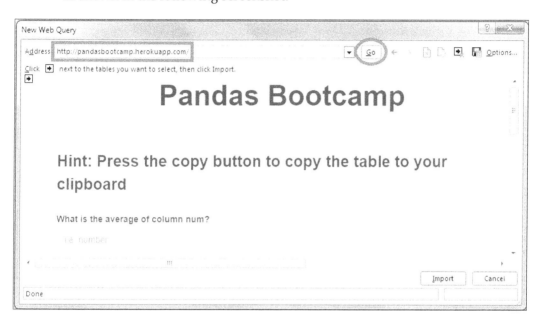

You will notice that in several places, on the website, you can see a yellow
square with a single back arrow, as shown in the following screenshot. This
button tells you that Excel has found a table on the website. This button also
tells you that you can grab the contents of the table and import them into
your spreadsheet. What do we mean by saying that the website has a table
on it? This is outside the scope of this book, as the answer requires you to
know HTML. But for your reference, Excel looks for HTML `<table>` tags to
identify tables on a website.

3. Scroll down to the end of the web page and then click on the last button and **Import** button, as shown in the following screenshot. Why did we choose to select the last button and not the first one? In this example, there were two buttons to choose from. Sometimes, the button will be right next to the table that you are interested in, and at other times, you will have to complete the task by trial and error.

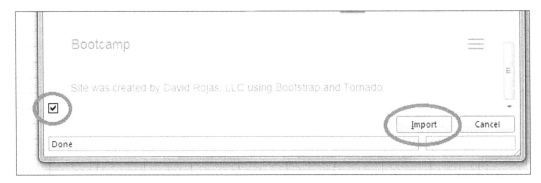

Notice that the yellow button will change to a green checkbox. After you click on the **Import** button, you will get a new dialog box that will ask you where you want to paste the data, as shown in the following screenshot. The cell **A1** is usually the default location selected, but you may change the location if you wish.

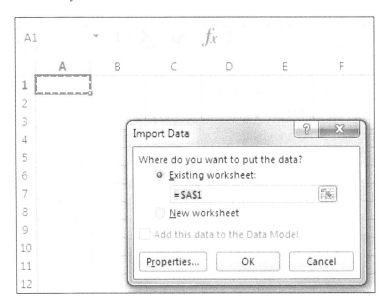

At this point, Excel will grab the data from the website, and you will have a worksheet that looks similar to the following screenshot. You should have 50 records, but they do not have to match the ones in the following screenshot:

	A	B	C	D	E
1	date	num	num2	str	str2
2	8/20/2015	392	569.658797	boy	yellow
3	9/8/2015	592	726.905288	girl	green
4	1/31/2015	99	724.342905	girl	yellow
5	1/19/2015	361	2.920015	girl	green
6	7/12/2014	603	828.063695	girl	yellow
7	7/4/2016	950	876.482364	girl	blue
8	8/23/2015	672	368.749061	girl	purple
9	1/4/2014	806	939.647914	boy	blue
10	2/8/2015	750	240.394564	girl	purple

Good job! You have just imported data from a website effortlessly, thanks to Excel's robust tools that helped you get the job done as easily and quickly as possible. The advantage of grabbing the data using the previous steps is that if there are any changes in the data on the website, we can easily update our spreadsheet to match any new changes. If we simply copy and paste the data from the website into Excel, we would have to perform these same steps every time the data changes. The *Pandas Bootcamp* website actually changes data every time you refresh the web browser. Try it!

This means that if we ask Excel to *refresh* or to check whether the website has any new data, it will update our spreadsheet with the new data. Let's give it a try.

4. Right-click on cell **A1** or any other cell with data. Go to the menu bar, and click on the **Refresh** button, as shown in the following screenshot. Your data should have changed! This feature will allow your data to always be in sync with just a few clicks.

Alternatively, we can perform this operation by hitting the **Refresh All** drop-down button under the **DATA** tab in Excel.

Summary

The lessons in this chapter were designed to teach you how to gather data from various data sources. You should now be able to pull data from text files, CSV files, other Excel files, and web pages. Getting data in your hands is the first step in the data analysis life cycle, and you now have the skills needed for this process. In the next chapter, we will take a look at the last set of data gathering skills that all data analysts should be equipped with. *Chapter 2, Connecting to Databases*, will guide you through detailed step-by-step instructions on how to connect to Microsoft SQL Server databases using Excel's data connection tools.

2
Connecting to Databases

In this chapter, we will continue our journey through the data analysis life cycle. We are still in the first step of the cycle and that is gathering data. I have dedicated a separate chapter to connect to databases as I feel that this topic is important and merits its own space. You will soon realize that a lot of data you work with is present in a database. Data, such as customer information, product information, log data, and a lot of information will be found in a database. Excel is a good introductory tool that you can use to get the data out of a database. Ultimately, learning how to query a database using one of the various flavors of **Structured Query Language** (**SQL**) should be your goal but until then Excel is your go-to tool.

In this chapter, we will read the various tables in a Microsoft SQL Server database. I have chosen the Microsoft SQL Server database because apart from Oracle, this is one of the most popular databases you will be interacting with.

Reading a table from MSSQL – the Microsoft SQL Server database

The data that we will import comes from a company called **Fast forms**. This company specializes in processing rental applications. Landlords or owners of homes sign up with Fast forms, and people interested in renting their homes can apply via the Fast forms' website. We will import the following table:

Users: This table holds information about all of the home owners who want to rent their homes. Data, such as their name, address, phone number, and registration date, will be found in the table.

1. Fire up Excel 2013 and create a new spreadsheet. Select the **DATA** tab, click on the **From Other Sources** button, and select the **From SQL Server** option, as shown in the following figure:

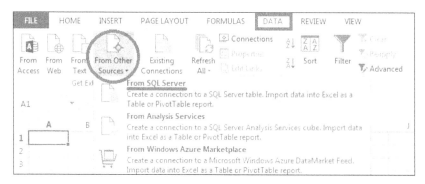

Figure 2.1

You will now see the **Data Connection Wizard** dialog box appear on the screen. Now, to connect to a SQL server database, you either need to have a local database available, or you need to make an attempt to connect to your clients'/companies' internal database. You may not have access to any of these options and that is fine. By following the given examples, you will be able to adapt to the examples presented in this chapter and read from databases in future. The data used in this chapter will be available in the Chapter 02 folder for your reference.

Figure 2.2

2. Type the name of your server and click on the **Next** button, as shown in the following screenshot. If your server requires a username and password, then you need to type these in the **Log on credentials** section, but 99 percent of the time, people tend to keep the default option of **Use Windows Authentication** selected, and click on the **Next** button. **Use Windows Authentication** means that you do not have to provide any usernames or passwords and Windows will take care of granting you access.

Figure 2.3

Where do I find the server name in a Microsoft SQL Server database?

In the following screenshot, you will find a dialog box that contains the name of the server. This dialog box is not found in Excel, but it is found in a different program called Microsoft SQL Server Management Studio. This program allows you to manage and query SQL Server databases. If you do not have access to this program, you will have to ask your client or coworker for the name of the server. Providing more information on Microsoft SQL Server Management Studio is outside the scope of this book, so we've not covered it here.

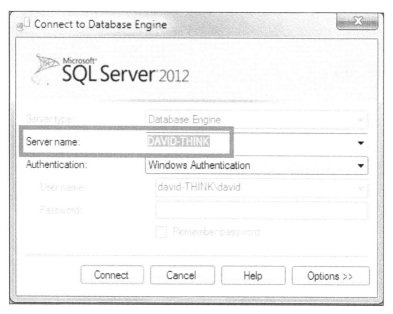

Figure 2.4

3. The next step in the **Data Connection Wizard** dialog box is to select the database, which contains the data that we want to import. If you are not familiar with the term database, do not be discouraged. A database is a collection of tables, functions, and other **database** objects. In this section, our goal is to import the table named **users**, and this table is located in the database called **BizIntel**. So, we proceed by selecting **BizIntel** in the drop-down menu, highlighting the **users** table under the **Column Name**, and clicking on the **Finish** button, as shown in the following screenshot:

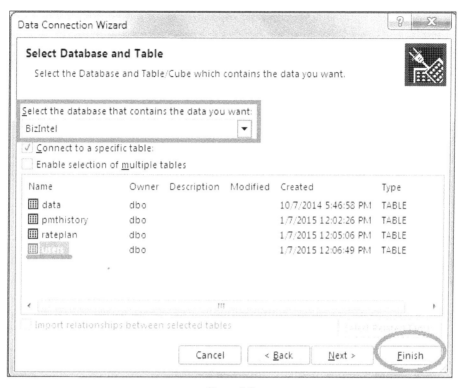

Figure 2.5

I am using a personal database, and you would most likely not have a database named **BizIntel** or a table named **users**. But you are now familiar with database terms, such as **table** and **database**, so you will be able to use these steps as a guide to your own data.

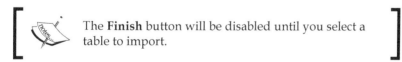 The **Finish** button will be disabled until you select a table to import.

4. After you click on the **Finish** button, you will get a new dialog box asking you where you want to place the data we are importing from the **users** table. We will keep the default location of cell **A1** and click on the **OK** button.

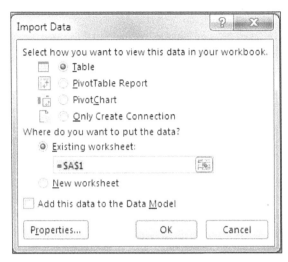

Figure 2.6

Congratulations! You have just queried a Microsoft SQL Server database and placed the results in an Excel spreadsheet. The steps that you just performed might not seem that interesting, but these steps have just given you the power to gather an unlimited amount of data. Think about it; earlier the data was stuck in a database and you couldn't do anything with the data. Now that you have learned how to get the data out of a database and into a familiar tool, such as Excel, you no longer have to be afraid of databases. You will now see that databases are wonderful sources of valuable data to consume and analyze.

Reading multiple tables from MSSQL

In this section, you will learn how to read multiple tables. In practice, the data that you will need will span multiple tables and is usually not found in a single table. We will import the following tables:

Users: This table holds information about all of the home owners who want to rent their homes. Data, such as their name, address, phone number, and registration date, will be found in this table.

PmtHistory: This table captures the data after a user applies to a rental property. It includes information, such as the date the application was submitted and the ID number of the property.

Rateplan: This table contains information on how much it costs the owner of the rental property to process an application.

1. We already know from the *Reading a table from MSSQL – the Microsoft SQL Server database* section how to import a single table, and we will repeat a lot of these steps but with a few differences. Make sure that you close Excel and open a new workbook. Select the **DATA** tab, click on the **From Other Sources** button, and select the **From SQL Server** option, as shown in *Figure 2.1* of the *Reading a table from MSSQL – the Microsoft SQL Server database* section.

2. Type the name of your server and click on the **Next** button, as shown in *Figure 2.3* of the *Reading a table from MSSQL – the Microsoft SQL Server database* section. If you do not know the name of your server, refer to the *Reading a table from MSSQL – the Microsoft SQL Server database* section for more information.

3. In the **Data Connection Wizard**, make sure that you select the **Connect to a specific table** and the **Enable selection of multiple tables** options.

Figure 2.7

4. Now, select the database that holds the tables named **users**, **pmthistory**, and **rateplan** by using the drop-down menu. In this example, the database is called **BizIntel**, and we select this option.

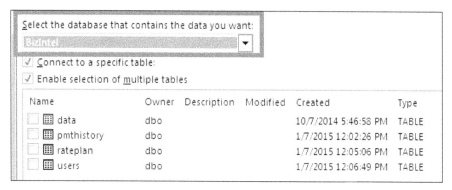

Figure 2.8

After selecting the database, you will see the **users**, **pmthistory**, and **rateplan** tables appear in the middle of the dialog box. Do not worry about the fourth table that shows up, which is named **data**. This is just an additional table that we can import into Excel if we choose to do so.

5. Select the three tables named **users**, **pmthistory**, and **rateplan**, as shown in the following screenshot. This action tells Excel that you want to import these specific tables. You have the option of choosing one or more tables in this step.

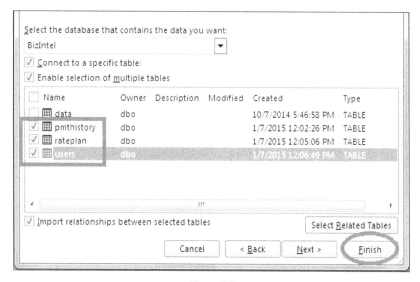

Figure 2.9

6. You will now see the **Import Data** dialog box with the **PivotTable Report**
    option selected by default. Select the **Table** option and click on the **OK**
    button, as shown in the following screenshot:

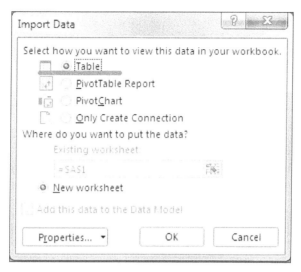

Figure 2.10

After you click on the **OK** button, each table will be placed in a separate
sheet. The sheets 2, 3, and 4 will contain the data in the tables named **users**,
pmthistory, and **rateplan**. That's it! You have just completed the *Reading
multiple tables from MSSQL* section.

Reading from MSSQL using SQL

This section will briefly show you how to use the SQL syntax to query a Microsoft
SQL Server database. In the previous two sections, we imported all the tables into
Excel and this was done easily. The issue is that we may only want a slice of the data
that is found in a table. We may also have a table that has 5 million rows and imports
large amounts of data that can cause Excel to crash. Even if we are able to import
large amounts of data, unless you really need all that information, you will spend
a lot of time to remove the excess data and waste time. A better idea is to edit any
existing connections that Excel has with the database via SQL queries. This is exactly
what we will learn in the *Reading a table from MSSQL – the Microsoft SQL Server
database* section.

What exactly are SQL queries? SQL is just a language that databases understand. It is a language used to give instructions to a database. Using this language, you can tell a database to grab the **users** table, but only the records where the **firstname** column is equal to **Mike**. So, instead of grabbing all of the records found in the **users** table, you can only grab records where the first name is **Mike** and life is good. Learning SQL is outside the scope of this book, but we will briefly introduce you to the language. It is important for you as a data analyst to be aware of SQL and see how you can use it with Excel. In practice, most of the data-gathering steps will most likely be performed with database-specific tools, such as Microsoft SQL Server Management Studio. After the data to be analyzed is gathered, it will then be moved to Excel for further analysis and reporting.

If you are still confused about SQL and what this actually means, do not worry as this is normal. The following steps will walk you through an example that will clear up some of the questions you are currently wrestling with:

1. We will create a data connection that is similar to the *Reading a table from MSSQL – the Microsoft SQL Server database* section. Select the **DATA** tab, click on the **From Other Sources** button, and select the **From SQL Server** option, as shown in *Figure 2.1* of the *Reading a table from MSSQL – the Microsoft SQL Server database* section.

2. Type the name of your server and click on the **Next** button, as shown in *Figure 2.3* of the *Reading a table from MSSQL – the Microsoft SQL Server database* section. If your server requires a username and password, you need to type these in the **Log on credentials** section. However, 99 percent of the time, you will keep the default option of **Use Windows Authentication** selected, and then click on the **Next** button. **Use Windows Authentication** means that you do not have to provide any usernames or passwords and Windows will take care of granting you access. Refer to *Figure 2.3* of the *Reading a table from MSSQL – the Microsoft SQL Server database* section.

3. The next step in the **Data Connection Wizard** dialog box is to select the database, which contains the data that we want to import. In this section, our goal is to import the table named **users** and this table is located in the database called **BizIntel**. So, we proceed by selecting **BizIntel** in the drop-down menu, highlighting the **users** table under the **Name** column, and clicking on the **Finish** button, as shown in *Figure 2.8*.

4. After you click on the **Finish** button, you will get a new dialog box asking you where you want to place the data that we are importing from the **users** table. We will keep the default location of cell **A1** and click on the **OK** button, as shown in *Figure 2.6* of the *Reading a table from MSSQL – the Microsoft SQL Server database* section.

In the *Reading a table from MSSQL* section of this chapter, you will now see that your data in **Sheet 1** has four records. For reference, you can find the data references in this section in a file named `users.csv` in the `Chapter 02` folder. In the following steps, we are going to edit the data connection so that it only returns records where the **firstname** column is equal to **Mike**. The following screenshot shows you a snapshot of the data:

	A	B	C	D	E
1	id	ip	propertyname	firstname	lastname
2	1	10.220.202.80	property1	David	Rojas
3	3	10.226.67.253	property2	Bob	Rojas
4	2	10.220.202.80	property3	Mike	Stuff
5	4	10.93.15.240	property4	Mike	Stuff

Figure 2.11

5. Select the **DATA** tab and select any cell in the table that we just imported in order to activate it. Click on the **Properties** button, as shown in the following screenshot. If you do not select a cell in the table, the **Properties** button will not be activated and you will not be able to click on the button.

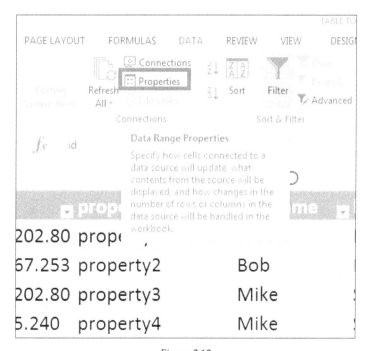

Figure 2.12

6. When the **External Data Properties** dialog box appears, click on the
   Properties button in the **Connection** section.

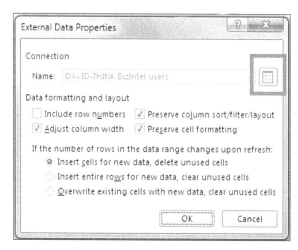

Figure 2.13

7. Select the **Definition** tab. This is where we are going to edit our data
   connection and enter our SQL query. But before we do this, let's take a
   closer look at the connection string in the following screenshot. There is
   a lot of information here, but I only want to point out a few key parameters.
   They are as follows:

   ○ **Data source**: The data source is the name of your server. It is the
     name of the server that we connect to and we discussed this in the
     Reading a table from MSSQL – the Microsoft SQL Server database section.

   ○ **Catalog**: The parameter named catalog refers to the name of the
     database. In our specific example, the catalog is set to **BizIntel**.

Another section worth mentioning is the **Connection file** section. Every time you create a data connection, Excel will save a file on your computer with all of the connection details. This means that the next time you open Excel, you will be able to use any of the data connections you created in the past. If you ever need to delete a connection, just click on the **Browse...** button and delete the connection of your choice. It will have a file extension of .odc and a filename that matches the **Connection name**.

Figure 2.14

8. Change the **Command type** from **Table** to **SQL**, as shown in the following screenshot:

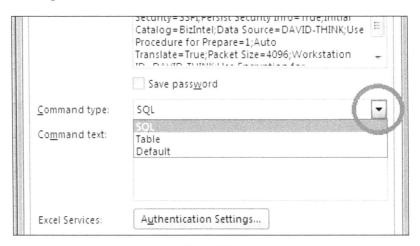

Figure 2.15

9. Clear any text in the **Command text** section and type the following SQL statement:

```
SELECT * FROM users
WHERE firstname = 'Mike'
```

The quotes around the word `Mike` can be single or double quotes, as shown in the following screenshot:

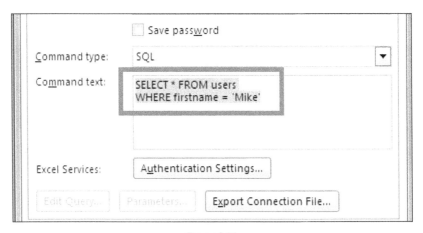

Figure 2.16

10. Now, click on the **OK** button, and your data in **Sheet 1** will get updated. If you get a dialog box similar to the one in the following screenshot, just click on the **Yes** button to continue.

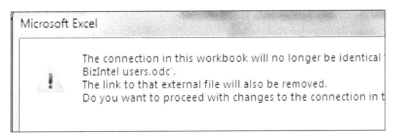

Figure 2.17

To finish applying the updates, click on the **OK** button on the **External Data Properties** dialog box, as shown in the following screenshot:

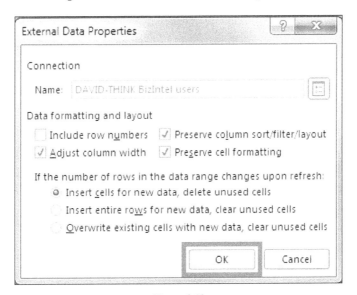

Figure 2.18

You will now only see two records and these are the ones with **Mike** as their first name. As you learn more about the SQL language, you can create more sophisticated queries. This concludes the *Reading from MSSQL using SQL* section and the chapter as well. Good job in blazing through the material. I guarantee you that this is valuable information that will serve you well in your data adventures.

Summary

The sections in this chapter were designed to teach you how to connect to a Microsoft SQL Server database using Excel's data connection tools. You will be able to gather data from one or many tables in a database. We also covered how to leverage SQL and selectively pull just the data we are looking for into Excel. In the next chapter, we will get acquainted with the next stage of the data analysis life cycle, that is, preparing your data.

3
How to Clean Texts, Numbers, and Dates

The first two chapters dealt with the first stage of the data analysis life cycle, the data gathering stage. In this chapter, we will get our hands dirty with steps that some people may want to avoid altogether. This is the stage that will challenge you creatively and intellectually and check your patience. Getting the data and then preparing it for a report or an analysis can be very time consuming. I remember working on a project that I was very excited about; I had just read a book about data mining and I was very eager to apply some of the knowledge that was still fresh in my mind. At that time, I was working for a book wholesaler, a company that purchased and sold college text books. My goal was to gather historical prices of books and predict when a book's price would go up or would go down. Just imagine that if this was possible, I could tell my boss which books to buy today or later because I could "predict" the future price of each book. It was a bold challenge and I took it up. The first step that I took should be familiar to you by now: gathering the data. I had to get as much historical data as I could, so I started the journey of gathering data. Data came to me on a monthly basis, so I started collecting monthly data files. I soon realized that there was data missing for some months. I then reached out to some of my coworkers and asked them, "Do you have the file for the month of February?" This gathering process alone took weeks and then I realized a demoralizing fact. The monthly file actually got updated up to four times by a third-party within that month. Yes, this meant that if I really wanted to do a good job, I needed the last file that received an update for a particular month. This file would have the most accurate data. To be honest, I did not get the most updated file per month because I did not want to spend months tracking down data, but I did as much as I could. By the end of the project, I was able to capture data that encompassed three years of book prices. Once the data is collected, we move on to the next stage, preparing the data. To analyze the data, we have to merge all the monthly files into one big file, and this is what the current chapter is all about, preparing our data for analysis.

While cleaning your data, you will find plenty of roadblocks, and in the following sections, you will find strategies to deal with them.

Leading/trailing/in-between spaces

There are times when your cells will contain leading spaces, trailing spaces, or extra spaces in between strings. These are issues that can lead you to draw incorrect conclusions about your data. Let's perform the following steps to create some data:

1. Fire up Excel 2013 and create a new spreadsheet. In columns **A** and **B**, enter the following information:

```
Product, Sales
   red apples, 10
red    apples, 10
red apples   , 10
```

By applying some of the concepts that you learned in *Chapter 1, Getting Data into Excel*, you should be able to reproduce a table, as shown in the following figure. Note that I have made the column headings **bold** and applied a border around the cells.

	A	B
1	**Product**	**Sales**
2	red apples	10
3	red apples	10
4	red apples	10

Figure 3.1

Another important fact about this data is that I added two extra spaces to cells **A2**, **A3**, and **A4**. In cell **A2**, I added the spaces before the word **red**. In cell **A3**, I added the spaces in between **red** and **apples**. In cell **A4**, I added the spaces after the word **apples**.

If I were to ask you to give me the total sales of **red apples** based on the data in columns **A** and **B**, what would your answer be? Correct, it would be 30. This is called aggregating data. You can also group the data by the **Product** column and sum up the **Sales** column. If we do so, we will get something similar to the following screenshot:

Figure 3.2

We can accomplish this in Excel by using a pivot table. This is the first time that we are creating a pivot table, so let's take it one step at a time.

2. Select cells **A1** through **B4**, click on the **INSERT** tab, and then click on the **PivotTable** button, as shown in the following screenshot:

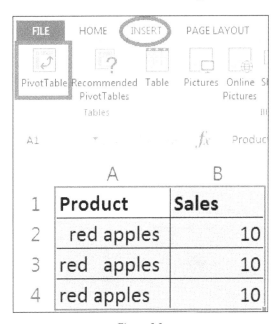

Figure 3.3

3. You will now get the **Create PivotTable** dialog box. In the section labeled **Choose where you want the PivotTable report to be placed**, select **Existing Worksheet**.

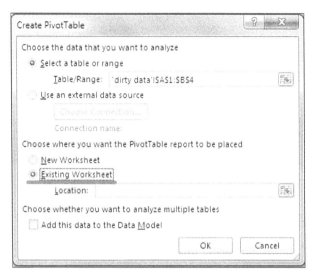

Figure 3.4

4. In the **Location** textbox, type E1 and click on the **OK** button, as shown in the following screenshot. You can also select cell **E1** by clicking on the **Location** button, which is located to the right of the textbox.

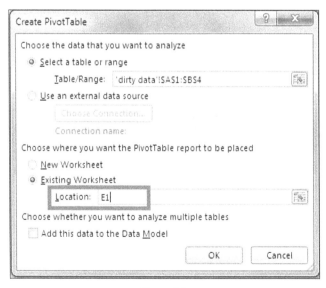

Figure 3.5

You will now get a window similar to the one in the following screenshot:

Figure 3.6

As you can see, **PivotTable Fields** correspond to the columns of the dataset that we created earlier. Don't worry about the bottom part of the screenshot, as we will cover pivot tables in depth later.

5. Click on the **Product** and **Sales** checkboxes, as shown in the following screenshot:

Figure 3.7

You will now see your pivot table appear in cell **E1**, as shown in the following screenshot. You have just completed your very first pivot table. Congratulations!

E	F
Row Labels	**Sum of Sales**
red apples	10
red apples	10
red apples	10
Grand Total	**30**

Figure 3.8

You might not see an issue in the previous screenshot, but there is a big problem here. Yes, the **Grand Total** is correct and the total **Sum of Sales** reflects **30**; however, the issue here is that there are three instances of the label **red apples**. What we want here is something similar to *Figure 3.2* of this section. There should only be one instance of the label **red apples**.

Now, this may seem silly, but when you are working with lots of data, these types of issues can slip through the cracks and may ruin your analysis.

So, how do we deal with spaces? Excel comes to the rescue by providing us with functions to clean up our data.

6. The most basic way to clean up our data is to do it manually. To be honest, if you have a small amount of data, it will not take you too much time, and there is nothing wrong with manually correcting the data issues. To do this, start by selecting cell **A2** and editing the string in the formula bar, as shown in the following screenshot. Delete the two extra spaces in front of the word **red**.

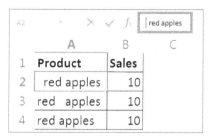

Figure 3.9

You can also edit the string in cell **A2**, but I have found out that it is easier to do so in the formula bar. Try editing the data in the cell and formula bar and decide for yourself which one you're more comfortable with.

Excel has a built-in function called **trim** that will remove these annoying spaces for you automatically. The advantage of using formulas is that you can apply them to any number of cells. This is the first time that we are writing formulas, so pay attention. We will create a new **Product** column and place it in between columns **A** and **B**.

7. Select the entire column **B** by clicking on the column **B**, as shown in the following screenshot:

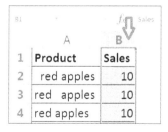

Figure 3.10

8. Right-click on the column **B** and select the **Insert** option.

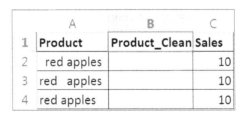

Figure 3.11

You have just created a space for our new column, which we will call **Product_Clean**. Use the following screenshot as a reference. Make sure that you label the column, as shown in the following figure:

	A	B	C
1	Product	Product_Clean	Sales
2	red apples		10
3	red apples		10
4	red apples		10

Figure 3.12

9. In cell **B2**, type =trim(and select cell **A2**, and then press the *Enter* key on your keyboard.

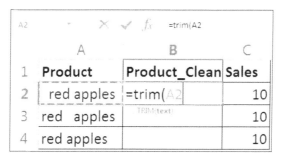

Figure 3.13

Cell **B2** will now have the same contents as cell **A2** minus any extra spaces. In other words, it removed the extra leading spaces that are in cell **A2**.

10. Now, let's apply this function to the other two cells. Select cell **B2** and move your mouse to the bottom-right corner of the cell. You will see that your mouse pointer changes to a **+**, as shown in the following screenshot:

	A	B	C
1	**Product**	**Product_Clean**	**Sales**
2	red apples	red apples	10
3	red apples		10
4	red apples		10

Figure 3.14

11. Now, drag the bottom-right corner of cell **B2** until you get to cell **B4**. You will now see that column **B** gets populated, as shown here:

	A	B	C
1	**Product**	**Product_Clean**	**Sales**
2	red apples	red apples	10
3	red apples	red apples	10
4	red apples	red apples	10
5			

Figure 3.15

You can also double-click on the + icon and Excel will automatically apply the formula to all of the cells.

Congratulations! You have just cleaned column **A** using formulas, bringing you closer to becoming an adept Excel developer. Note that column **A** still has issues, but our new column **B** should have removed any extra spaces and corrected the issue. Now, let's recreate the pivot table using our new column and check whether we have corrected our data issue.

12. Select cells **B1** through **C4**, click on the **INSERT** tab, and then click on the **PivotTable** button.

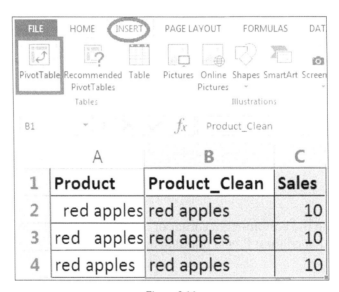

Figure 3.16

13. In the **Create PivotTable** dialog box, under the option called **Choose where you want the PivotTable report to be placed**, type **F8**, as shown in the following screenshot:

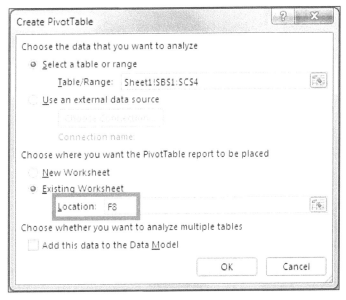

Figure 3.17

14. Navigate to the right of your screen and check the column boxes labeled **Product_Clean** and **Sales**.

Figure 3.18

You will now see your final PivotTable in cell **F8**, as shown in the following screenshot:

Row Labels	Sum of Sales
red apples	30
Grand Total	**30**

Figure 3.19

As you can see, we now get only one instance of the label **red apples**. Good job!

Capitalization

You might find yourself receiving data that is not consistently capitalized. The following steps will help you quickly capitalize your cells:

1. Fire up Excel 2013 and create a new spreadsheet. In column **A**, enter the following information:

    ```
    Name
    david Rojas
    Bill Fergus
    Mary blue
    BOB BOBBY
    MikE HoPe
    ```

    The following is some sample data that comes from an online registration form.

	A
1	**Name**
2	david Rojas
3	Bill Fergus
4	Mary blue
5	BOB BOBBY
6	MikE HoPe

    Figure 3.20

    As you can see, some of the names are capitalized and some are not. We also have some names that are all in caps and others that have capital letters in odd places. In practice, these inconsistencies come from web forms or user-created spreadsheets. Excel has a very handy function called **proper** that will correct all of these issues in a flash.

2. In cell **B2**, type =PROPER(and select cell **A2**, and then press the *Enter* key on your keyboard, as shown in the following screenshot:

    Figure 3.21

3. Copy the same formula to the rest of the cells, as shown in steps 10 and 11 of the *Leading/trailing/in between spaces* section. You will now get results that are similar to the following screenshot:

	A	B
1	**Name**	
2	david Rojas	David Rojas
3	Bill Fergus	Bill Fergus
4	Mary blue	Mary Blue
5	BOB BOBBY	Bob Bobby
6	MikE HoPe	Mike Hope

Figure 3.22

As you can see, Excel consistently capitalized all of our strings even though they were all over the board previously. All it took was to use one simple formula and we were done. I'm hoping that you will understand the value of formulas and how they can help you in your data analysis adventures.

Duplicates

Duplicate data is something that you will be dealing with over and over again. If it has not become a habit to check for duplicates, then start getting used to it. Excel has useful tools to help you identify and remove duplicate data.

1. Fire up Excel 2013 and create a new spreadsheet. In cell **A1**, enter the following information:

    ```
    Color
    blue
    blue
    red
    green
    ```

You will now have a spreadsheet that looks like the following screenshot:

Figure 3.23

Our goal is to remove any duplicates in our data using Excel's built-in functionality. I know that this is a very simple example but remember that the same steps can be applied to large amounts of data as well.

2. Highlight cells **A1** through **A5**, select the **DATA** tab, and click on the **Remove Duplicates** button.

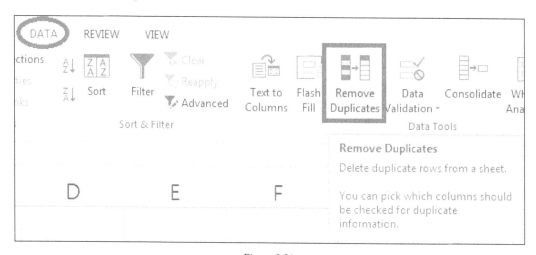

Figure 3.24

3. When the **Remove Duplicates** dialog box appears, click on the **OK** button, as shown in the following screenshot:

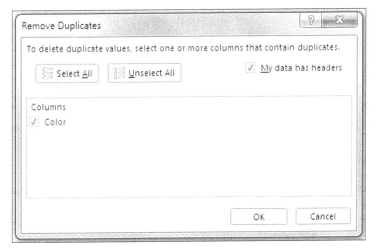

Figure 3.25

Excel will then remove any duplicates that it finds and column **A** will look like this:

Figure 3.26

You will also get a summary of how your data was changed.

Figure 3.27

If you do not want Excel to change your original data, make a
copy of your data in another column and remove the duplicates
from the new column.

Text to Columns

There are times you might get data so that when you open Excel or when you paste
the data into Excel, it all shuffles into the first column. Intuitively, you know that the
data has multiple columns but it just gets stuck in one column. Excel comes to the
rescue by using a tool named **Text to Columns**. You can perform the following steps
to get some hands-on experience using this feature of Excel:

1. Fire up Excel 2013 and create a new spreadsheet. In cell **A1**, enter the
   following information:

   ```
   Product, Sales

   red apples, 10

   red apples, 10

   red apples, 10
   ```

2. With cells **A1** through **A4** selected, press the following keys on your
   keyboard one after the other *Alt + O + C + A*. This keyboard command will
   auto resize the highlighted cells so that you can clearly see the text on the
   screen. Your spreadsheet will now look like the following screenshot. This
   also confirms that our data is in column **A**.

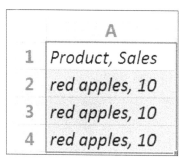

Figure 3.28

3. With cells **A1** through **A4** selected, navigate to the **DATA** tab, and click on
   the **Text to Columns** button.

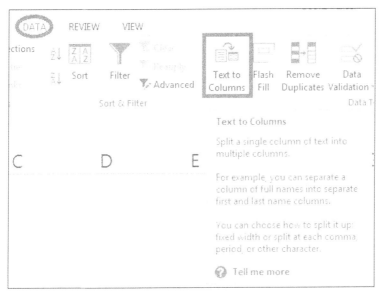

Figure 3.29

4. You will now see the **Convert Text to Columns Wizard** dialog box appear on the screen. From *Chapter 1, Getting Data into Excel*, you will realize that this dataset is delimited or separated by a comma. Click on the **Next** button, as shown in the following screenshot:

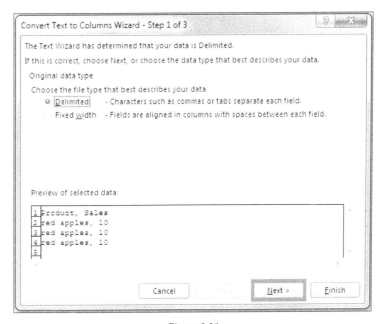

Figure 3.30

5. When the **Convert Text to Columns Wizard** dialog box appears, uncheck the **Tab** checkbox, select the **Comma** checkbox, and then click on the **Finish** button.

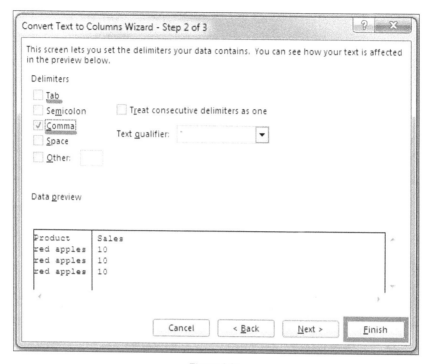

Figure 3.31

You will now have data that looks similar to the following screenshot. Now, you are done! It was that easy to convert text into columns using Excel's powerful toolset.

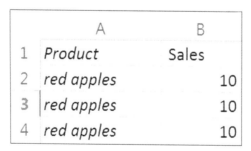

Figure 3.32

Combine data from multiple columns into one column

Sometimes, you will find data in multiple columns but you would want to combine this data into one column. Some examples are the names of people and their addresses. Here, we can use an Excel function to combine or concatenate the strings together:

1. Fire up Excel 2013 and create a new spreadsheet. In columns **A** and **B**, enter the following information:

    ```
    First Last
    David Rojas
    Bill Fergus
    Mary Blue
    Bob Bobby
    Mike Hope
    ```

    You will have a dataset similar to the one in the following screenshot:

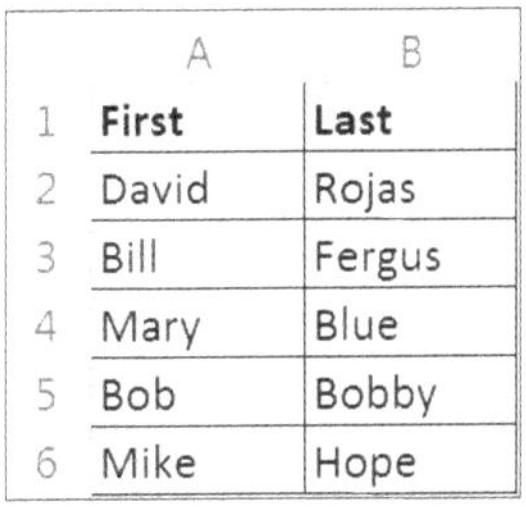

	A	B
1	**First**	**Last**
2	David	Rojas
3	Bill	Fergus
4	Mary	Blue
5	Bob	Bobby
6	Mike	Hope

    Figure 3.33

2. In cell **C2**, type = and then click on cell **A2**.

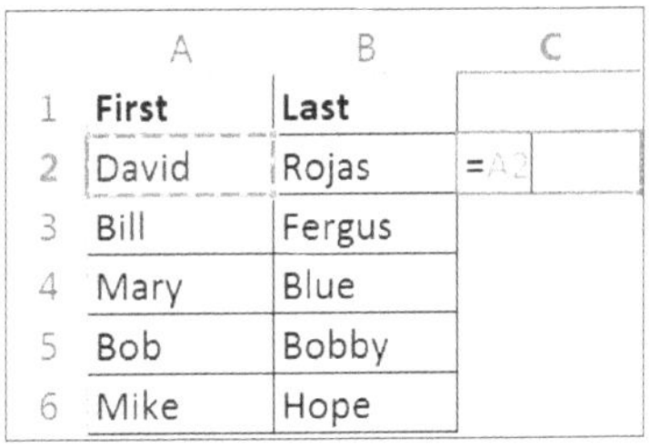

	A	B	C
1	**First**	Last	
2	David	Rojas	=A2
3	Bill	Fergus	
4	Mary	Blue	
5	Bob	Bobby	
6	Mike	Hope	

    Figure 3.34

3. Now, type & and click on cell **B2**.

	A	B	C
1	First	Last	
2	David	Rojas	=A2&B2
3	Bill	Fergus	
4	Mary	Blue	
5	Bob	Bobby	
6	Mike	Hope	

Figure 3.35

Press the *Enter* key on your keyboard, and you will now see that cell **C2** gets populated, as shown in the following screenshot:

	A	B	C
1	First	Last	
2	David	Rojas	DavidRojas
3	Bill	Fergus	

Figure 3.36

Do you see an issue with cell **C2** in the previous screenshot? Yes, of course, there is a space missing in between the first and last name. We can correct this by modifying our formula in the formula bar:

4. Select cell **C2** and click inside the formula bar.

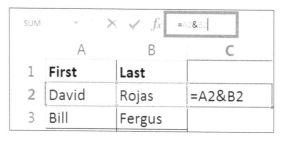

Figure 3.37

5. Change the formula for the text, as shown in the following screenshot:

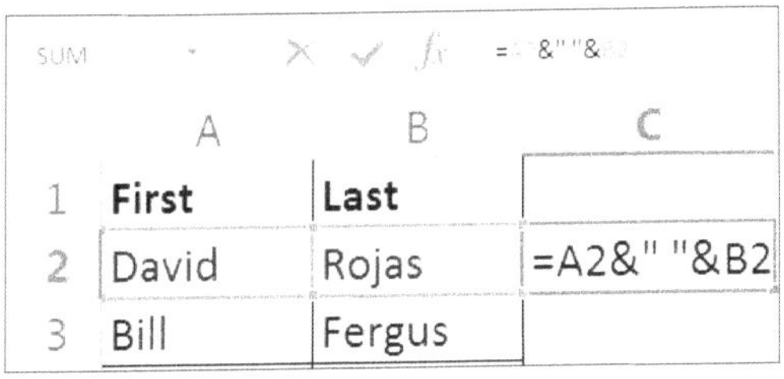

Figure 3.38

The ampersand (**&**) character glues the strings together, as shown in steps 3 and 4. Then, we used two double quotes with a space in between them to create a space in between the first and last name. The final output will look like this:

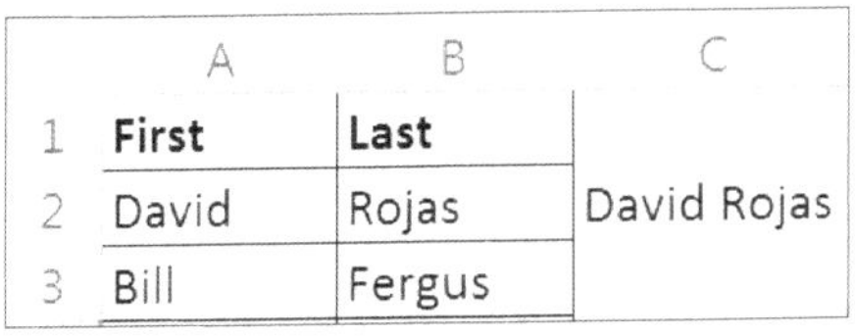

Figure 3.39

You can now try to apply the same formula to the rest of the cells in column **C**, as we did in steps 10 and 11 of the *Leading/trailing/in between spaces* section.

Fixing similar words

Words that are spelled similar to the original word is another common issue that we have to face when analyzing data. Addresses are notorious for being spelled in many ways. Your goal is to make your data as consistent as possible before you begin to do any analysis. In the following steps we will use **filters** to tackle this issue:

1. Fire up Excel 2013 and create a new spreadsheet. In column **A**, enter the following information:

```
String
123 Mill Street
123 Mill St.
123 Mill Str
#2 Electronic Store
#22 Electronic Store
#13 Electronic Store
```

You will have a dataset that is similar to the one in the following screenshot:

Figure 3.40

2. Click on the top-left corner of your spreadsheet, which is in between column **A** and row **1**, as shown in the following screenshot:

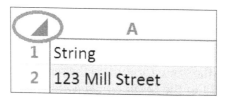

Figure 3.41

This will highlight every cell and row of your spreadsheet.

 Even though we only have data in one column, it is recommended that you select the entire worksheet before you apply a filter to your data. The advantage is that the same steps can be performed regardless of the amount of data you are working with.

3. With your data selected, navigate to the **DATA** tab and click on the **Filter** button, as shown in the following screenshot:

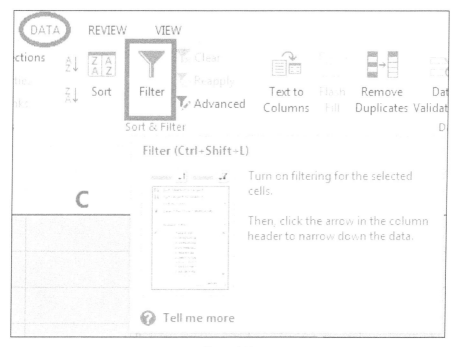

Figure 3.42

 You can also turn the filter on and off by pressing *Ctrl + Shift + L* on your keyboard. Remember to highlight your data before you attempt this shortcut.

4. Click on the drop-down button that appears on the column heading named **String**, select the **Text Filters** menu option, and then click on the **Contains...** option.

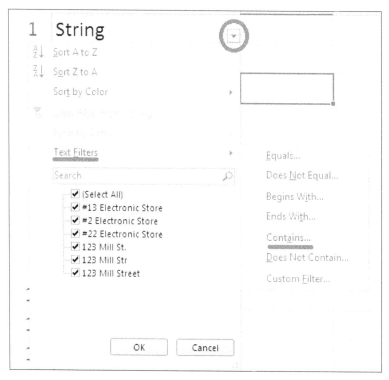

Figure 3.43

5. In the **Custom AutoFilter** dialog box, type 123 Mill into the textbox.

Figure 3.44

Let's pause for a second to review what we are doing here. The purpose of steps 4 and 5 is to filter our data. We want to filter our data so that only the three instances of **123 Mill Street** appear. We cannot use the word **street** because this word is spelled differently. Instead, we use the other words that they have in common, **123 Mill**. So, this is the reason why in step 5, we use the string **123 Mill**.

We will now get the three records, as shown here:

Figure 3.45

With the records, we want to standardize in focus, we can simply modify them so that they are all identical. You can use the copy/paste method or manually modify the text by using the formula bar. When you are done with editing the three cells, you will have something that looks like the following screenshot:

Figure 3.46

6. Select the entire worksheet, as shown in step 2, and click on the **Filter** button, as shown in step 3. You will now be able to see your entire dataset, as shown in the following screenshot:

Figure 3.47

This was basically the strategy for this section. As you can see, we cleaned up half of our data using filters. You can also perform the same steps to clean the **Electronic Store** strings. Give it a try before moving on to the next section.

Text to dates

Dates are one of those words that can either make you smile or make you frown. In the past I have had many issues dealing with dates but without them, I would not be able to answer the questions I was tasked with. One of the most common issues is having your dates formatted as strings. In Excel, if your dates are treated as strings, any formulas that are meant for date cells will fail. The following steps will help you get around this issue:

1. Open the spreadsheet in the Chapter 03 folder named Chapter 3 - Lesson 7.xlsx.

   You will have a dataset that is similar to the one in the following screenshot:

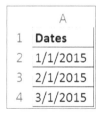

Figure 3.48

Notice that we added a single quote in front of the strings to trick Excel into thinking that these are strings and not dates.

2. Select cell **A2** and press *Ctrl + 1* on your keyboard. You will get a dialog box telling you what the data type of cell **A2** is, as shown in the following screenshot. It says that the cell is of the **General** category. This basically means that it treats the cell as a text field. We then need to convert these text fields into the **Date** category.

Figure 3.49

3. Select the category named **Date** and then click on the **OK** button on the dialog box. You have just converted cell **A2** from a text field or data type into a date field. Note that cell type, field type, and data type all mean the same thing. You can also select multiple cells and press the *Ctrl + 1* keys to convert the remaining cells into dates.

4. Now, type =day(A2) into cell **B2**, =month(A2) into cell **C2**, and =year(A2) into cell **D2**. I also went ahead and added column labels (**Dates, Day, Month,** and **Year**), as shown in the following screenshot:

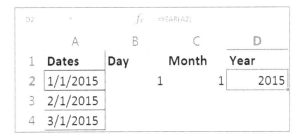

Figure 3.50

Text to numbers

Receiving numerical data formatted as string is another common issue that we need to take care of. If your formulas are not working and your calculations are giving you incorrect results then it is time to make sure your numerical cells are not formatted as strings.

1. Open the spreadsheet in the `Chapter 03` folder named `Chapter 3 - Lesson 8.xlsx`.

   You will have a dataset similar to the one in the following screenshot. The following steps will show yosu how to convert the text values in column **A** into numbers.

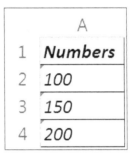

Figure 3.51

2. Select cells **A2** through **A4** and click on the yellow exclamation button, as shown in the following screenshot:

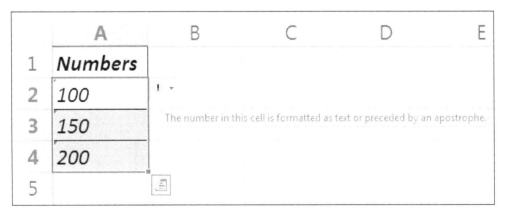

Figure 3.52

3. In the drop-down menu, click on the **Convert to Number** option.

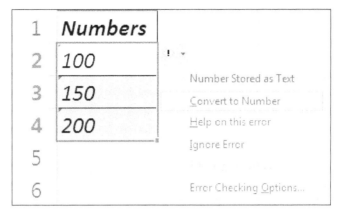

Figure 3.53

That's pretty much all there is to it; you have just converted text into numbers. Good job!

Summary

We covered many of the common data issues that you might encounter when working with data and several strategies to deal with them. Every dataset will have its own challenges that go well beyond what we have covered so far, but by the end of this chapter, you would be able to handle a good number of scenarios. What you can bet on is having data quality issues which will force you to clean your data. As we saw time and time again, Excel has plenty of built-in tools that will ease your pain and make your life a lot easier. In the next chapter, we will continue to focus on how to prepare our data but we will take it to the next level. Advanced uses of formulas and conditional statements are introduced with simple-to-follow examples.

4
Using Formulas to Prepare Your Data for Analysis

We continue with stage three of the data analysis life cycle, preparing your data for analysis. We covered formulas in *Chapter 3*, *How to Clean Texts, Numbers, and Dates*, but we will make sure that you know Excel's formulas inside out. In the Excel world, formulas are used to perform data transformations. Formulas allow you to make many changes to many cells in a short period of time. In the previous chapter, we had a set of strings that needed to be capitalized in a consistent manner. Now, even though there were only around five records, we could have easily manually edited the cells, but we chose to use a formula. We typed the formula into one cell, and then Excel allowed us to easily copy the formula to the other cells. Pause for a second. Suppose that we had 15,000 records and not just five. We could have just applied the formula to 15,000 records. This is where the power of Excel's formulas comes from. In the following steps, we will continue practicing how to build formulas to add to your skill set.

How to create formulas

What exactly are Excel formulas? These are pieces of code that are typed into a cell and always start with an equals sign. The equals sign (=) tells Excel that you are about to create a formula in that cell. Let's create some simple formulas:

1. Fire up Excel 2013 and create a new spreadsheet. In cell **A1**, enter the following formula:

   ```
   =5+5
   ```

The following screenshot shows you cell **A1** before you press the *Enter* key on your keyboard. After pressing the *Enter* key, you will see a value of 10 in cell **A1**.

2. Delete the contents of cell **A1** and enter the following formula in cell **A1**:

    ```
    =hello world
    ```

    After you press the *Enter* key, you will get a similar result, as shown in the following screenshot:

The goal of the preceding formula was to enter a string in cell **A1**, but it did not work. Cell **A1** should have the value **hello world**, but it does not. What just happened here? **#NAME?** means that there is an error in your formula. When we enter strings in a formula, we have to place quotes around the string so that Excel accepts the formula. Let's make this change to our formula.

3. Delete the contents of cell **A1** and enter the following formula in cell **A1**:

    ```
    ="hello world"
    ```

    Now, you will not get an error message and cell **A1** will look like the following screenshot:

Combining strings and numbers

In this section we will cover how to enter numbers, strings, and how to combine both of these data types into a single cell. I encourage you to practice while you are reading as the more time you invest in practice the more formulas will become second nature.

1. Fire up Excel 2013 and create a new spreadsheet. Manually enter the following information:

	A	B	C	D
1	String1	String2	Number	Combined
2	I am	years old.	20	

    Our goal is to create the following phrase in cell **D2**:

    I am 20 years old.

2. In cell **D2**, type = and then select cell **A2**, as shown in the following screenshot. Do not press the *Enter* key.

A2		✕ ✓ *fx*	=A2		
	A	B	C	D	
1	String1	String2	Number	Combined	
2	I am	years old.	20	=A2	

3. Continue with the formula that we started with in the previous step by typing &C2&B2.

	A	B	C	D
1	String1	String2	Number	Combined
2	I am	years old.	20	=A2&C2&B2

    After you press the *Enter* key on your keyboard, you will get **I am20years old**. However, this is not exactly what we wanted. Think about what we need to do. Yes, we need to add spaces before and after the number **20**. We can add spaces by entering two double quotes with a space in between them. Let's make this happen in the next step.

4. Delete the contents of **D2** and type the following formula in cell **D2**:

    ```
    =A2&" "&C2&" "&B2
    ```

Your cell **D2** will look similar to the following screenshot:

	A	B	C	D
1	String1	String2	Number	Combined
2	I am	years old.	20	=A2&" "&C2&" "&B2

Notice that in the formula, each cell identifier gets a different color. Excel uses this feature to help you pinpoint where a specific cell is located. For example, in the preceding figure, cell **C2** is colored red and, in **D2**, cell **C2** is also colored red. This is a very useful feature but be aware that the more cells you reference in a formula, the harder it will be for you to make use of the color feature.

Nevertheless, cell **D2** will now read **I am 20 years old.**, and you now know how to add spaces in between the strings. You have also realized that Excel can handle both combining text and numeric input without any extra considerations.

Using built-in functions

Excel comes with a vast amount of handy formulas that we do not have to create from scratch. These formulas range from data cleaning to financial formulas a CPA may use on a daily basis. In this section we will cover some of the common ones every Excel developer should be aware of.

1. Fire up Excel 2013 and create a new spreadsheet. Manually enter the following information:

	A	B	C
1	String	Find $	Remove $
2	$David		
3	Da$vid		
4	David$		

The goal of *this exercise* is to remove the $ character from the **String** column. We will use two Excel functions to accomplish this task:

2. In cell **B2**, type =find("$",A2), as shown in the following screenshot. Note that this search is case sensitive.

B2		X	✓	*fx*	=find("S",A2)	

	A	B	C
1	**String**	Find $	Remove $
2	$David	=find("$",A2)	
3	Da$vid		
4	David$		

The `find` function will look for a string within a string. If it finds a match, it returns the integer position of the location. The first parameter asks us to enter the string that we are looking for. In our case, it is the dollar sign. The second parameter asks us to enter the location of the string that we will be searching for. In our case, the location is cell **A2**. There is a third parameter as well, but it is optional, so we will ignore it for the time being.

After you press the *Enter* key on your keyboard, you will get a value of **1** in cell **B2**, as shown in the following screenshot. What does this mean? This means that the character **$** was found in cell **A2** in position **1**.

	A	B	C
1	**String**	Find $	Remove $
2	$David	1	
3	Da$vid		

3. Now, copy the formula to cells **B3** and **B4**, and you will get results that are similar to the following screenshot. Now that Excel knows the location of the string that we want to remove, let's now make use of the function called `replace`.

	A	B	C
1	**String**	Find $	Remove $
2	$David	1	
3	Da$vid	3	
4	David$	6	
5			

4. In cell **C2**, type =replace(A2,B2,1,""), as shown in the following screenshot. The first parameter **A2** is the string from which we want to remove some characters. The second parameter **B2** is the location of the character that we want to remove. Remember that we were able to find the location of **$** by using the find function in column **B**. The third parameter asks us for the number of characters to be replaced, and in our case, this would be one. The fourth and last parameter tells you what to replace the **$** character with. We chose two double quotes with nothing in between them. This basically just means that you should replace **$** with nothing, or in other words, remove the **$** character.

SUBSTITUTE ▾	✕ ✓ *fx*	=REPLACE(A2,B2,1,"")		
	A	B	C	D	E
1	**String**	Find $	**Remove $**		
2	$David		1	=REPLACE(A2,B2,1,"")	
3	Da$vid		3	REPLACE(old_text, start_num, num_chars, new_text)	
4	David$		6		

5. Copy the formula from cell **C2** and apply it to cells **C3** and **C4**. You will get the same results.

	A	B	C
1	**String**	Find $	**Remove $**
2	$David	1	David
3	Da$vid	3	David
4	David$	6	David
5			

If/else/then statements

Conditional statements is our next topic at hand. This functionality will give you, the Excel developer, more control, power, and freedom. You will now be able to add intelligence to your spreadsheets and the following examples will tell you how to do this:

1. Fire up Excel 2013 and create a new spreadsheet. Manually enter the following information:

	A	B	C	D
1	Fruit	Inventory	Buy	How Many?
2	Apples	200		
3	Grapes	50		
4	Pears	150		
5	Bananas	175		

Column **B** tells us how much inventory we currently have on hand. In column **C**, we will determine whether we need to buy more inventory. Column **D** will tell us whether we have to buy more inventory and how much inventory we have to buy. We are going to make the assumption that we cannot have more than 200 items in our inventory. In other words, we cannot have more than 200 apples, 200 grapes, and so on.

How are we going to determine whether we are low in inventory? We are going to use Excel's conditional statements.

2. In cell **C2**, type =if(B2<200,"yes","no"), as shown in the following screenshot. How does the if function work? The first parameter is a conditional statement. The second parameter yes is what happens if the conditional statement is true. The third parameter no is what happens if the conditional statement is false. In our case, we want to know if we have less than 200 apples in the inventory. If we have less than 200 apples, we will write yes in cell **C2**. If we have 200 or more apples, we will write no in cell **C2**. Note that we make the assumption that anything less than 200 means low in inventory.

SUBSTITUTE	✕ ✓ *fx*	=IF(B2<200,"yes","no")		
	A	B	C	D
1	Fruit	Inventory	Buy	How Many?
2	Apples	200	=IF(B2<200,"yes","no")	
3	Grapes	50	IF(logical_test, [value_if_true], [value_if_false])	
4	Pears	150		
5	Bananas	175		

3. Apply the same formula to cell **C2** and to the rest of the cells in column **C**. Can you guess which cells will say **yes** and which cells will say **no**? You will get similar results, as shown in the following screenshot:

	A	B	C	D
1	Fruit	Inventory	Buy	How Many?
2	Apples	200	no	
3	Grapes	50	yes	
4	Pears	150	yes	
5	Bananas	175	yes	
6				

Congratulations! Your spreadsheets are now smart and can make decisions on their own. If you change any value in column **B**, column **C** will automatically update it. Try it out for yourself!

4. If we are low in inventory, we will have to decide how much fruit to buy. Also remember that the maximum amount of fruit that we can buy is 200, so we have to make sure that we do not exceed 200. In cell **D2**, type =if(C2="yes",200-B2,0), as shown in the following screenshot:

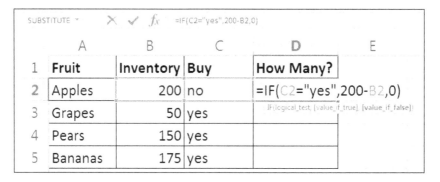

5. Apply the same formula to the rest of the cells in column **D**. You will get similar results, as shown here:

	A	B	C	D
1	Fruit	Inventory	Buy	How Many?
2	Apples	200	no	0
3	Grapes	50	yes	150
4	Pears	150	yes	50
5	Bananas	175	yes	25

Do the results in column **D** make any sense? It tells you not buy any apples, as we already have a maximum inventory amount of 200 apples. The spreadsheet then asks us to buy 150 grapes. This makes sense as we only have 50 in the inventory and by adding 150 to it, this will bring the total to 200 grapes. Buying 50 pears will bring the total inventory of pears to 200. Adding 25 bananas to the 175 that we already have in the inventory will bring the total to 200. If we take a look at the data, we can see that column **A** correctly tells us what fruit we need to buy and column **D** has the correct amount of fruit to be purchased. As you can see, we can add values to our data by applying a few conditional formulas.

Comparing columns

A very common use of if/else statements is to compare two columns and determine whether there are any differences. For example, let's say that we have inventory data that comes from two different sources. One can be from a report and the other can be from the data that comes from the accounting department. The report data and the data from the accounting department do not match.

At this point, we are not sure who is correct or incorrect but all we know is that they are different. Our task is to find out what the differences are and then create a report on them. The following steps will show you how to complete this task:

1. Fire up Excel 2013 and create a new spreadsheet. Manually enter the following information:

	A	B	C	D	E
1	Date	Report Inventory		Date	Accounting Inventory
2	1/1/2015	564		1/5/2015	2
3	1/2/2015	59		1/4/2015	3
4	1/3/2015	8		1/3/2015	8
5	1/4/2015	2		1/1/2015	564
6	1/5/2015	3		1/2/2015	59
7	1/6/2015	8		1/10/2015	6
8	1/7/2015	684		1/9/2015	65
9	1/8/2015	4		1/8/2015	4
10	1/9/2015	65		1/7/2015	684
11	1/10/2015	9		1/6/2015	8

On the left-hand side, we have the inventory data from a report. On the right-hand side, we have the inventory data from the accounting department.

2. The first step is to sort both the sets of information by date. Highlight cells **A1** through **B11**, select the **DATA** tab, and click on the **Sort** button.

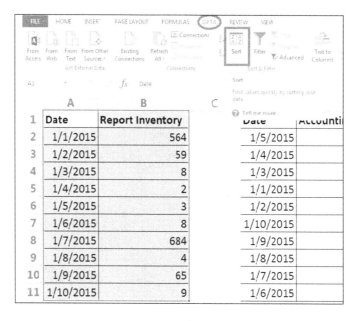

3. In the **Sort** dialog box, sort the data by **Date** and click on the **OK** button, as shown in the following screenshot. Nothing has changed as the data was already sorted correctly but just to get into the habit, it is better not to assume that the data is sorted correctly.

4. Perform steps 2 and 3 on cells **D1** through **E11**. You will now have two sets of data that are sorted identically. This means that you can now compare them by applying the same techniques that we learned in this chapter.

5. In cell **C2**, type `=if(B2=E2,"pass","fail")`, as shown in the following screenshot. After you press *Enter*, you will get **pass** in cell **C2** as both cell **B2** and cell **E2** have a value of **564**.

6. Apply the same formula to cell **C2** and to the rest of the rows in column **C**. You will now be able to clearly see where the differences between the two sets of data lie.

	A	B	C	D	E
1	Date	Report Inventory		Date	Accounting Inventory
2	1/1/2015	564	pass	1/1/2015	564
3	1/2/2015	59	pass	1/2/2015	59
4	1/3/2015	8	pass	1/3/2015	8
5	1/4/2015	2	fail	1/4/2015	3
6	1/5/2015	3	fail	1/5/2015	2
7	1/6/2015	8	pass	1/6/2015	8
8	1/7/2015	684	pass	1/7/2015	684
9	1/8/2015	4	pass	1/8/2015	4
10	1/9/2015	65	pass	1/9/2015	65
11	1/10/2015	9	fail	1/10/2015	6

We can see that rows **5**, **6**, and **11** are the data points that we are interested in. These are the rows where the inventory numbers do not match between columns **B** and **E**. The key for this analysis, apart from gathering the data, was to align both the datasets. We did this using Excel's sorting capabilities. After our data was sorted, we were then able to use formulas to identify any discrepancies. I hope you learned a lot in this section.

Summary

The main idea of the sections that we covered was to get you used to writing formulas and to let you know that there is nothing to be afraid of. We took baby steps in our initial sections and then took bigger and bigger steps in each subsequent section. We were able to use some of Excel's built-in functions to clean our data and got a good feel for the conditional formulas. I hope that you were blown away by the if/else/then statements presented in the later sections in this chapter. From entering data to developing intelligent spreadsheets, we have covered a lot of ground in a short amount of chapters. In *Chapter 5, Analyzing Your Data Using Descriptive Statistics and Charts*, we will use the knowledge from the previous chapters and finally get started with analyzing data.

5
Analyzing Your Data Using Descriptive Statistics and Charts

We are finally at that step of the process for which we've been waiting for: the analysis step. This is the step where we put our inquisitive hat on and start to get to know the data we are working with. This is the step where you can uncover new information and possibly find more data issues. We will go through the actual data from a website called Fast Forms. This is a website for people who rent property and for those who are looking to rent their property. What kind of data does this website have? Is it the data that tracks web visitors? No, the data does not consist of those who have visited the site; the data comes from the web application's own database. You will have to continue to read this chapter to find out more information. Note that we will be going through the same steps we have already covered in addition to introducing basic statistics and plotting. This is one of the chapters that will utilize a lot of the concepts and skills that you have learned so far, so I am sure that you'll enjoy it.

Gathering data

This part is going to be easy because the data has already been gathered, and it is available in the folder named `Chapter 05`. It contains three CSV files, and each file represents a specific table in the database.

Open each of the three files and familiarize yourself with the columns and data found inside:

- `Pmthistory.csv`
- `Rateplan.csv`
- `Users.csv`

Note that in order to get this data out of the database, we will have to either perform steps similar to the ones in *Chapter 2, Connecting to Databases,* or use some other means. So, how did I get this data? The data is present in the Postgres database, and I used Python to retrieve the data and save it in CSV files. It is also important to mention that I own and run this website.

Preparing the data for analysis

The next steps involve opening each CSV file and inspecting each of them for any potential issues. I will give you some background information about each table and how they fit in relation to the Fast Forms website:

1. Open the file named `users.csv`. The first thing that you might notice is that some of the cells are cut off. In other words, in some of the cells, the content does not fit and only some part of the data is visible, as shown in the following screenshot:

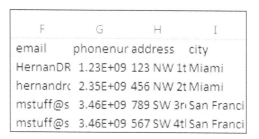

Figure 5.1

As you can see, the column named **email** is not wide enough to show the data in that column. The same situation occurs in the **address** column. Column **G** holds the numeric information and it is also not wide enough. Excel adds some interesting scientific notations to the cells, but this really means that the column is not wide enough to show all of the data inside the cells.

To resolve this issue, we can simply perform the following steps:

1. Highlight the entire worksheet by clicking on the button in between row **1** and column **A**, as shown in the following screenshot:

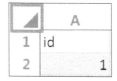

Figure 5.2

2. Navigate to the **HOME** tab, click on the **Format** button, and select the **AutoFit Column Width** option.

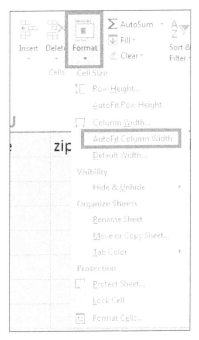

Figure 5.3

 You can also use the keyboard shortcut, *Alt + O + C + A,* to adjust the width of the selected cells.

Now, you will have all your data visible and this will look similar to the data in the following screenshot:

	F	G	H
	email	phonenumber	address
	HernanDRojas@gmail.com	1234567890	123 NW 1th RD
	hernandrojas@gmail.com	2345678901	456 NW 2th RD
	mstuff@someplace.com	3456789012	789 SW 3rd Dr
	mstuff@someplace.com	3456789012	567 SW 4th Dr

Figure 5.4

The biggest thing to notice here is that column **G** looks very different from the same column in *Figure 5.1* of this section. This is something that just comes with Excel and something you should be aware of.

2. Now that we can see all of our data, let's take a look at each column one by one. Scroll to the column named **ID**. The **ID** column is a numeric column that spans from 1 to 4. It is not sorted in ascending order or descending order but this may not matter to us. What does the **users** table mean? What is the point of this table? The users table holds all of the information of Fast Forms' customer base. These are all of the people who pay money to Fast Forms for its services. They are the owners of apartments and/or condos that they want to put up for rent. When one of these property owners signs up with Fast Forms, they have to fill out an online form and their information is entered into the **users** database. In our example, we have four records in our database; but in reality, there are only three unique customers. Note that rows **4** and **5** belong to the same customer named **Mike Stuff**. Also, note that the data has been altered to protect the identity of the actual Fast Forms' customers. The **ID** column is the primary key of the table and this number will be used to identify specific customers in the database. Database concepts are out of the scope of this book but just note that you will never find duplicate data in a primary key column. In other words, the numbers in the **ID** column are all unique. In practice, how do you find out whether a column is a primary key or not? If you have access to the database software, you will be able to find this out easily. If you do not, then asking a coworker who may know is your best bet.

3. Scroll to the column named **IP**. This column was added to track the user's computer identification. We can see that the same computer entered rows **2** and **4**. This is a little odd since these two records have different names and are from different cities. This means that these two records were registered by the same computer. As a data analyst, you should look out for inconsistencies and point them out. I would need to find out who the owner of the database is and ask him to explain why rows **2** and **4** have the same IP address. Since I am the owner of this table, I can tell you that this column can be ignored. The IP addresses captured are not accurate, and I have had many issues trying to get them working correctly. So, in this case, we can simply ignore the IP column.

4. Scroll to the column named **PropertyName**. This column does not have to be unique as the data is entered by the property owner at the time of registration. So, it is possible to have different properties that have the same property name. This is why we need the **ID** column to uniquely identify a property.

5. Scroll to the columns named **FirstName** and **LastName**. Here, we can look for data that is not written consistently. This is important because if we do find inconsistent data, we have to clean it before we run any kind of analysis. All of the names are capitalized and the last two rows are from the same person. There is nothing unusual found here.

6. Scroll to the column named **Email**. The first thing that I noticed is that the first two rows have HernanDRojas@gmail.com capitalized differently. Our goal is to have the data as similar and consistent as possible. Going forward, I would most likely change all the strings in this column to lowercase.

7. Scroll to the column named **PhoneNumber**. The phone numbers include the area code and do not have any dashes or parentheses. I would expect the first two rows to have the same phone number but they don't. This may be a data issue or nothing at all, but it is something that you need to be aware of.

8. Scroll to the columns named **Address**, **City**, **State**, and **ZipCode**. The address of each record is broken up into individual pieces, which can be very useful for reporting purposes. I would expect to see all of the addresses to be different since each record pertains to a unique property.

9. Scroll to the column named **RatePlanID**. This column is a foreign key from another table called **RatePlan**. It is used to identify what rate plan a specific property is currently enrolled in. This will determine how much Fast Forms is going to charge the customer for using its services. All of the records have a value of one and there is really nothing more to do here.

10. Scroll to the columns named **EffectiveBeginDate** and **EffectiveEndDate**. The purpose of these columns is to let Fast Forms know whether the property is currently active or not. If the property is not active, then renters interested in renting the property will not be able to do so using the Fast Forms website. The property will essentially be disabled. For example, if today's date is May 1, 2015, then the **EffectiveBeginDate** will have to be on or before May 1, 2015 for the property to be considered active. If the **EffectiveEndDate** is populated, then it will have to be a date that comes after May 1, 2015 for the property to be considered active. If we take a look at column **M**, we can see that all four properties are currently active. The oldest property seems to be **property1** and the most recent property to enter the system seems to be **property4**.

11. Scroll to the column named **DateAdded**. This column tells us on which date the record was added to the database. We can tell that the first two records were added on the same day. It is very interesting to note that the **EffectiveBeginDate** for row **4** is before the **DateAdded** value.

As you can see, just by taking a glance at your data, you can begin the analysis process and start gathering insights. We also looked for possible data issues and places where we have to do some data cleansing. Let's continue with the second table called `rateplan.csv`.

12. Open the file named `rateplan.csv`, as we did in steps 1 to 3, and adjust the cell widths so that you can clearly see all of your data. You will now see data similar to the following screenshot:

A	B	C	D	E	F	G	H	I	J
id	name	price	limit	default	lockedin	signupexp	effbegindate	effenddate	dateadded
1	default	1		1		1/1/2099	1/1/2014	1/1/2099	3/27/2014
2	free	0				1/1/2099	1/1/2014	1/1/2099	3/28/2014

Figure 5.5

The **RatePlan** table will store all of the rate plans a customer can be enrolled in. How Fast Forms works is that every time someone applies to be a renter at one of your properties, you are charged a fee. This **fee** is determined by your rate plan. For example, if you are enrolled in the **default** rate plan, you will get charged $1 for every application that is submitted through Fast Forms. How did we know it was $1? If we take a look at *Figure 5.5*, we can see that the first row corresponds to the **default** plan and the column named **price** determines how much to charge the customer. Makes sense?

13. Scroll to the column named **ID**. This is the primary key of the table and it is used to uniquely identify a rate plan.

14. Scroll to the column named **Name**. This column will hold unique names for each rate plan, but we will most likely use the **ID** column to identify the rate plans. Note that these records were created by the database developer (me) and are not known by any of the users of Fast Forms.

15. Scroll to the column named **Price**. From the introduction, we should already be familiar with this column. We know that we should treat the values in this column as numbers and not strings.

16. Scroll to the column named **Limit**. This column caps the total number of applications a property can process under the rate plan. If the limit is 10, then only ten applications can be processed for a property with this rate plan. This was added as a convenience for Fast Forms users. Some of our customers may only want to spend or receive a certain number of applications. Fast Forms can then create a custom rate plan to fit their needs. This column is empty, so the data analyst does not have to worry.

17. Scroll to the column named **Default**. This column tells us that when someone signs up with Fast Forms and wants to rent his/her property, then by default, he/she will be put on the **default** rate plan. This information is valuable for reporting purposes. Suppose that you were asked to find all the customers who were not in the default rate plan. You would know how to identify these customers using the **rateplan** table and **default** column.

18. Scroll to the column named **LockedIn**. This means that if a customer is currently on a rate plan that is **lockedin**, he/she will need special permission to switch to another rate plan. Normally, customers who are on a rate plan that has expired will automatically get rolled over to the default rate plan. This will not happen if they are in a **lockedin** rate plan. This information I just shared with you is called **domain knowledge**. You either have it, or you need to ask someone who has it. This is the reason why it is very important to be in contact with the database developer of the data you are analyzing.

19. Scroll to the rest of the date columns.

20. The **SignUpExp** column is where the last date to sign up for the rate plan is present.

21. The **EffBeginDate/EffEndDate** column is the date range the rate plan is active for.

22. The **DateAdded** column is the date on which the record was added to the database.

23. If we take a look at the dates in the preceding screenshot, it seems that none of the two rate plans will expire anytime soon.

24. Open the file named pmthistory.csv. As we did in steps 1 to 3, adjust the cell widths so that you can clearly see all of your data. You will now see data similar to the following screenshot:

id	ip	userid	rateplanid	status	dateadded
8	10.185.0.100	50		FALSE	6/6/2014
9	10.185.157.183	1	1	TRUE	6/6/2014
10	10.42.121.33	3	1	TRUE	7/9/2014
11	10.123.47.121	3	1	FALSE	7/10/2014
12	10.228.25.238	3	1	FALSE	7/10/2014

Figure 5.6

This table keeps a record of every application submitted through Fast Forms. This table is very important because this table tells Fast Forms who owes them money and how much money. Fast Forms uses this table to bill their customers.

25. Scroll to the column named **ID**. This column is the primary key of the table, but it has no real meaning to us. We can simply ignore this column.

26. Scroll to the column named **IP**. As mentioned in step 5, this column contains bad data and should be ignored. It was originally placed here to identify *bad guys* or people trying to do bad things to the Fast Forms website.

27. Scroll to the column named **UserID**. This is a foreign key that points to the table named **users** from step 1. It tells us that someone submitted an application to this property. Notice that there is a **userid** of value **50**, and I do not remember the **users** table having a row with this value. Do you remember? Also, notice that the **rateplanid** column is null. This may be some bad data that you need to be aware of.

28. Scroll to the column named **RatePlanID**. This is a foreign key to the table named **rateplan** from step 12. It basically tells us how much to charge our customers for the application that was submitted.

29. Scroll to the column named **Status**. This is a very important column because it tells us whether the application was submitted successfully. If it was not submitted successfully, then we do not charge the customer.

30. Scroll to the column named **DateAdded**. This column tells us the date on which the application was submitted.

We took a look at our data, searching for any inconsistencies, outliers, and data issues. We defined each column we were working with and understood how each of the three tables related to each other. We also got a glimpse of how a website such as Fast Forms is powered by data. In the next section, we will go even deeper and answer key questions about our data.

Analyzing our data

We will be posing questions about our data that will force us to generate descriptive statistics and make use of Excel's plotting features to come up with answers. These are typical questions that you will get when analyzing or reporting on data.

Question – how many applications were processed in the year 2014?

Make sure that the data is broken down by month. Use the `pmthistory.csv` file as your data source:

1. Fire up Excel 2013 and create a new spreadsheet. Copy the contents of the `pmthistory.csv` file and paste them into **Sheet 1** of your new spreadsheet.

2. Create a pivot table that counts the number of applications submitted in a month. To do this, we need to create a custom date column. Make a new column called **month**, as shown in the following screenshot. In cell **G2**, type 6/1/2014 and press the *Enter* key on your keyboard.

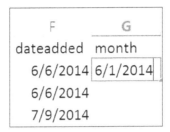

Figure 5.7

What are we trying to do here? We want the **month** column to be a copy of the **dateadded** column, but we want all of the dates to be on the first of every month. We do this so that when we create our pivot table, we can group all of the applications that were processed in that month together. If we do not create a new column and use the column named **dateadded**, Excel will not know how to combine, for instance, the dates **7/9/2014** and **7/10/2014** in the same group.

3. Now, type **6/1/2014** in cell **G3** and press the *Enter* key on your keyboard, as shown in the following screenshot:

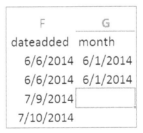

Figure 5.8

What we are about to do next will blow you away; we are going to use a new Excel 2013 feature that will auto-fill the remaining rows for you. Excel will take a look at what we have done so far in cells **G2**/**G3** and try to figure out the pattern. It will then proceed and fill in the rest of the cells in column **G** with its guesses. So, how do you tell Excel to make a guess? The next step will give you the answer.

4. Press the *Ctrl + E* keys and Excel will auto-populate the rest of the columns. Excel magically knows that all you are doing is copying the same date, as shown in the **dateadded** column, but changing the date to the first of each month. If Excel guessed this wrong, then all you have to do is press the *Ctrl + Z* keys to undo and give Excel more data to work with. You can enter 7/1/2014 in cell **G4** and then press the *Ctrl + E* keys to try again. The following screenshot shows you the results after Excel entered the values for us automatically:

Figure 5.9

5. Create a pivot table using the **month** and **ID** columns. If you need a refresher on pivot tables, refer to the *Leading/trailing/ in between spaces* section in *Chapter 3, How to Clean Texts, Numbers, and Dates*. We will place the pivot table in cell **E1**, the **month** column in the **ROWS** section, and the **id** column in the **VALUES** section, as shown in the following screenshot:

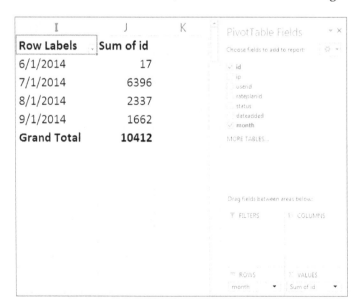

Figure 5.10

To quickly select all of the columns, highlight cells **A1** through **G1**, and press *Shift* + *Ctrl* + the down arrow key on your keyboard.

Note that the pivot table in cell **E1** sums up the values in the **ID** column. This is not correct as we want to count the values and not sum them up. Remember that our goal is to find out how many applications were submitted on each month in the year 2014. The next steps will correct this issue.

6. Select the **Sum of id** drop-down menu and select the **Value Field Settings...** option, as shown in the following screenshot:

Figure 5.11

7. Select **Count** in the **Value Field Settings...** dialog box and click on the **OK** button.

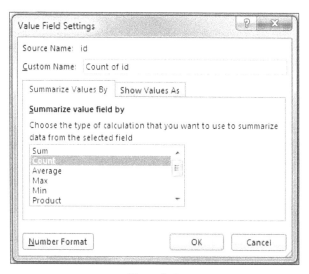

Figure 5.12

You will now have a pivot table that looks similar to the following screenshot:

Row Labels	Count of id
6/1/2014	2
7/1/2014	104
8/1/2014	19
9/1/2014	12
Grand Total	**137**

Figure 5.13

We can now answer the question "How many applications were processed in the year 2014?" The answer is 137. We could have also scrolled down to row 138 and come up with the same answer. We need to remember to remove one from 138 since the first row contains the column headers. Now the question also wanted us to break the counts per month and we have done this as well. We can see that there were only two applications processed in June and 104 in July. I wonder why July has so many applications and the other months have so few. Let's continue analyzing our data by visualizing it.

8. Select the entire pivot table minus **Grand Total**.

I	J
Row Labels	**Count of id**
6/1/2014	2
7/1/2014	104
8/1/2014	19
9/1/2014	12
Grand Total	**137**

Figure 5.14

9. Go to the **INSERT** tab and click on the **Recommended Charts** button, as shown in the following screenshot:

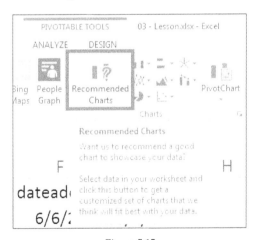

Figure 5.15

10. In the **Insert Chart** dialog box, we will stick to the default bar chart and click on the **OK** button.

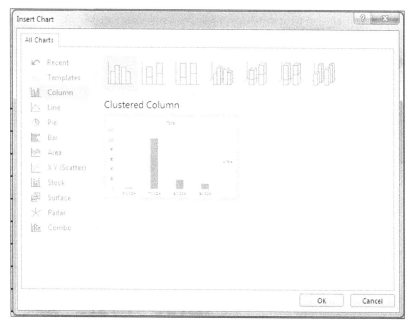

Figure 5.16

The chart will appear in the middle of your screen, but it comes in our way, so let's move it to another sheet.

11. Press the *Shift + F11* keys and this will create a new sheet named **Sheet2**. Now, click on the **Sheet1** tab to go back to our chart.

Figure 5.17

12. Select our chart by clicking on any empty space near the top of the chart. Make sure that you do not select any individual pieces of the chart such as the title or the axis. Press the *Ctrl + X* keys to cut the table from **Sheet1**.

13. Select the **Sheet2** tab, as we did in step 11, and press the *Ctrl + V* keys to paste our chart into the active sheet, as shown in the following screenshot. As you can see, Excel makes it very easy for you to create charts using our data. We just created a chart with our dates in the *x* axis and our counts in the *y* axis. From this chart, we can clearly see that the month of July had the most activities and the month of June had the least:

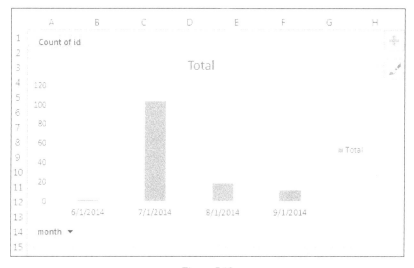

Figure 5.18

14. In addition to the chart, we can generate descriptive statistics about our data. Go back to **Sheet1**, navigate to the **DATA** tab, and select the **Data Analysis** option, as shown in the following screenshot:

Figure 5.19

15. In the **Data Analysis** dialog box, select the **Descriptive Statistics** option, and click on the **OK** button.

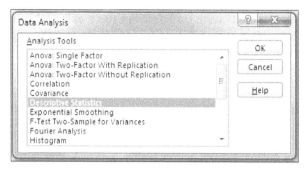

Figure 5.20

16. In the **Descriptive Statistics** dialog box, click on the **Input Range** button. This will allow us to choose our data.

Figure 5.21

17. Select cells **I1** through **J5** and press the *Enter* key on your keyboard, as shown in the following screenshot:

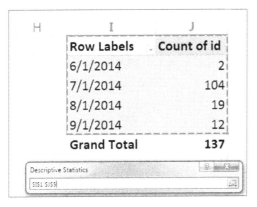

Figure 5.22

18. Make sure that both the **Labels in First Row** and **Summary Statistics** options are checked, as shown here:

Figure 5.23

19. Now, let's make sure that the results are placed in cell **L1**. Select the **Output Range** button to select your location, as shown in the following screenshot. Note that you have to select the radio button before you select your output range.

Figure 5.24

20. Select cell **L1**, as shown here:

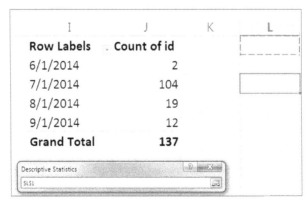

Figure 5.25

21. Press the *Enter* key on your keyboard, which will bring you back to the **Descriptive Statistics** dialog box, and then click on the **OK** button.

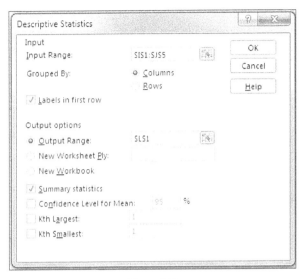

Figure 5.26

You will now get similar results in cell **L1** of **Sheet1**, as shown in the following screenshot:

L Row Labels	M	N Count of id	O
Mean	41836.75	Mean	34.25
Standard Error	19.81739556	Standard Error	23.51019282
Median	41836.5	Median	15.5
Mode	#N/A	Mode	#N/A
Standard Deviation	39.63479111	Standard Deviation	47.02038565
Sample Variance	1570.916667	Sample Variance	2210.916667
Kurtosis	-1.245906083	Kurtosis	3.581937939
Skewness	0.030126261	Skewness	1.867638487
Range	92	Range	102
Minimum	41791	Minimum	2
Maximum	41883	Maximum	104
Sum	167347	Sum	137
Count	4	Count	4

Figure 5.27

As shown earlier, we saw how Excel can automatically generate summary statistics about our data. We can ignore columns **L** and **M** as these hold our date data. It does not make any sense to calculate the average or the sum of the date values.

22. Delete columns **L** and **M** by selecting both the columns, right-clicking on your mouse, and selecting the **Delete** option.

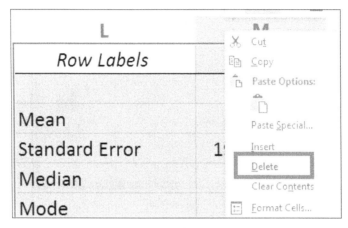

Figure 5.28

Let's go through some of the most useful summary statistics for the **count of id** column. We can start by asking ourselves whether the data is normally distributed. This means that the data looks like a bell-shaped graph. This is important because if it does not (like most datasets in practice), then you cannot use metrics such as the average and standard deviation. I repeat that the average and standard deviation are metrics that only apply to normally distributed data. We start by looking at our chart on **Sheet2**, and we can see that the peak is not really in the center and is more to the left of the chart. If we go back to **Sheet1** and take a look at the numbers for **Kurtosis** and **Skewness**, we can see that it does not look good for us. For our data to be normal, these two numbers have to be close to zero and they are not. This means that we will ignore the mean and standard deviation numbers as they do not apply. If we cannot use the mean, then what can we use? The median is your best choice for normally and not normally distributed data. So, if someone were to ask you on an *average* how many applications were submitted every month in the year 2014, you would say around 15. We do not say 15.5 because in our case, we do not count partially completed applications. Now, also understand that we only have four data points and having such little data does not help us make accurate statements. Other metrics, such as the maximum, minimum, and count, also help us understand our data. These metrics tell us how small and how large our data is. They also tell us how many data points we are working with. In our case, our data goes from 2 to 104 and we have a total of four data points.

The next set of questions you can start asking yourself is why does the month of July have so many applications? You can also take another look at the `pmthistory.csv` file and ask what do the rows with **userid** of 50 mean? Is it bad data? Did users of the Fast Forms website really enter a user ID that did not exist? Was it test data? There were also a lot of rows where the **status** column was **false**. This means that the application was not submitted successfully. Does this mean that there is an issue with the Fast Forms website or does it mean that users of the website are having trouble getting it to work? Another good question to ask is how much money did Fast Forms make in the year 2014? You already have all the information you need to figure this out. Give it a try and see if you can find out how much money Fast Forms made in the year 2014.

Summary

This chapter is one of my favorites because it brings so many concepts from the previous chapters together and shows you how everything fits together with the help of a simple example. We had to gather data, prepare data, and analyze data. Hopefully, you are beginning to see that analyzing data means that you need to ask lots and lots of questions. You also need to remember that domain knowledge is very important. You need to know the background of the data you are working with and how it fits into the bigger picture. You also realized that having a good eye for *bad* data is a skill that you need to tune over time. We also made use of pivot tables and charts to get more insights into our data. We also covered the steps needed to automatically generate descriptive statistics about our data in detail. These statistics helped us look deeper into our data and get a better feel of what we are working with. By the end of the chapter, you need to know your data inside and out. In *Chapter 6, Link Your Data Using Data Models*, we are going to make use of the new Excel 2013 features and learn how to combine multiple datasets into one. Having your data in one place will make your life easier and convenient for analysis and reporting. This chapter will empower you with sophisticated and advanced skills that will make you stand out from the crowd!

6
Link Your Data Using Data Models

This chapter will take us back to the data preparation stage. Sometimes, your data is in multiple places, and it will make your life easier if the data was present in one sheet. We will use Excel's data model feature to combine data from multiple sources into one. We will also discuss the database concepts but nothing too advanced. In terms of Excel, this new data model replaces the use of the well-known **VLOOKUP** function in some instances. We will merge the three datasets from the Fast Forms website that we learned about in *Chapter 5, Analyzing Data Using Descriptive Statistics and Charts*. Fasten your seat belts as the next few sections will come and go in a flash.

Gathering data

This part is going to be easy because the data has already been gathered and it is available in the Chapter 05 folder. It contains three CSV files and each file represents a specific table in the database.

1. Fire up Excel 2013 and create a new spreadsheet. Create two more tabs in addition to the **Sheet1** tab that has already been created for you by default. Rename **Sheet1**, **Sheet2**, and **Sheet3** as pmthistory, rateplan, and users, respectively, as shown in the following screenshot:

2. Copy the data from the three spreadsheets to their respective tabs:

    ○ `Pmthistory.csv` to the **pmthistory** tab

    ○ `Rateplan.csv` to the **rateplan** tab

    ○ `Users.csv` to the **users** tab

    You will now have 138 rows in the **pmthistory** tab, two rows in the **rateplan** tab, and five rows in the **users** tab.

     As an alternative, you can also use the **Move or Copy** sheet option that we learned in *Chapter 1, Getting Data into Excel*, to copy the data into a new workbook.

3. Create a new tab and call it `report`. Note that you can click and drag the tabs and reorder them in any way you want. In other words, you can move the **report** tab and place it first if you want.

4. Select the **pmthistory** tab and click on any cell with data in it. We are about to convert our data into an Excel table. This will allow us to make use of the data model features that I am so eager to show you. Press *Ctrl + T* and you will get a similar dialog box, as shown in the following screenshot:

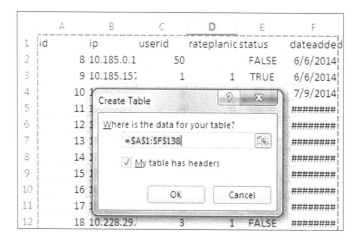

Excel will automatically select all of the columns and rows that have data. Click on the **OK** button in the **Create Table** dialog box or press the *Enter* key on your keyboard. It is really easy to convert your data and create an Excel table.

5. Select the **rateplan** tab and click on any cell with data in it. Convert the data into a table by pressing *Ctrl + T* followed by the *Enter* key on your keyboard.

6. Select the **users** tab and click on any cell with data in it. Convert the data into a table by pressing *Ctrl + T* followed by the *Enter* key on your keyboard.

7. Now, let's name our tables so that we can identify them when creating our pivot tables and data models. Select the **pmthistory** tab and click on any cell with data in it. In the top menu bar, find the **DESIGN** tab and select it.

8. On the top-left hand side of your screen, find the **Table Name:** option and change it from **Table1** to **pmthistory**, as shown in the following screenshot. Make sure that you press the *Enter* key on your keyboard so that the change in the table name is applied to your table.

9. We are now going to repeat step 8 in the other two tables. Select the **rateplan** tab and click on any cell with data in it. Click on the **DESIGN** tab and change the table name from **Table2** to **rateplan**. Make sure that you press the *Enter* key on your keyboard so that the change in the table name is applied to your table.

10. For the final table, select the **users** tab and click on any cell with data in it. Using step 9 as a reference, change the table name from **Table3** to **users**. Make sure that you press the *Enter* key on your keyboard so that the change in the table name is applied to your table.

Preparing data

Now that we have gathered our data, we can start asking questions of interest about our dataset. For example, we can ask how much money did Fast Forms make in 2014? To answer this question, we will start by using the well-known **VLOOKUP** function, and then, we will use the exciting new data model's features.

The **pmthistory** table has all of the applications that were submitted in 2014. It does not have the dollar amount that was charged to the customer. It does have a column named **rateplanid** and this column points to the table called **rateplan** that will tell us the dollar amount we are looking for. In the database world, the **rateplanid** column in the **pmthistory** table is known as a foreign key. The column **id** in the **rateplan** table is known as the primary key. Let's create a VLOOKUP function to pull the **price** column from the **rateplan** table into the **pmthistory** table:

1. Select the **pmthistory** tab and type price into cell **G1**, as shown here:

2. In cell **G2**, type =vlookup and then select cell **D2**. You will now get a formula that looks like the following screenshot. The first parameter asks us for the lookup value. These are the values we are trying to find in the column **id** from the **rateplan** table.

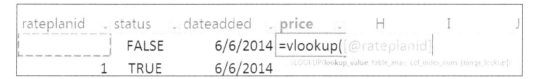

3. In cell **G2**, type a comma and select the **rateplan** table, as shown in the following screenshot. Note that after typing the comma, we have to select the **rateplan** tab, and with our mouse, we need to highlight all of the cells from the table.

 Since we have already named the table **rateplan**, you can just type rateplan rather than selecting the tab and highlighting the data in that table, in which case, the complete formula will look like this:

=VLOOKUP([@rateplanid],rateplan,3,FALSE)

4. Enter a comma on your keyboard and type 3, as shown in the following screenshot. The **col_index_num** parameter asks us for the location of the **price** column. If you take a look at the **rateplan** table, you can see that the **price** column is the third column from the left.

5. Enter a comma on your keyboard and a dialog box will pop up asking you to choose between **True** and **False**. Since we are looking for an exact match between the **rateplanid** column from the **pmthistory** table and the **id** column from the **rateplan** table, we need to choose **FALSE**. Remember to double-click on the **FALSE** option or type it manually. You can also type 0 for false and 1 for true.

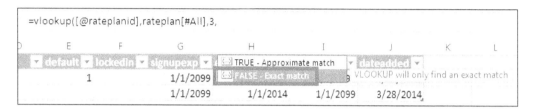

6. Make sure that you close the parentheses after step 5. Select the **pmthistory** tab if you are not already there. You will now have similar results in the **price** column, as shown in the following screenshot. Notice that Excel automatically filled in the entire **price** column even though we only created the formula in cell **G2**.

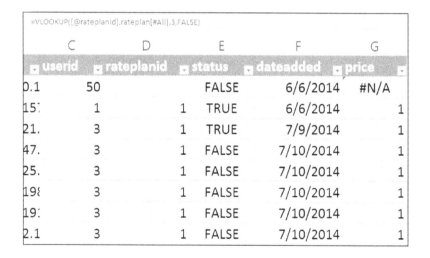

What does **#N/A** in cell **G2** mean? This just means that a match was not found between the two tables that we were trying to join. If you take a look at cell **D2**, you can see that it is blank and this is the reason we could not find a match.

Analyzing data

With our data, we can try to answer the question we posted in the *Preparing data* section of this chapter. We'll start by creating a pivot table and then create our data model that we have been promising:

1. Select the **pmthistory** tab and select any cell with data in it. Navigate to the **INSERT** tab and click on the **PivotTable** button.

2. In the **Create PivotTable** dialog box, select the **Existing Worksheet** option, and click on the **Location** button.

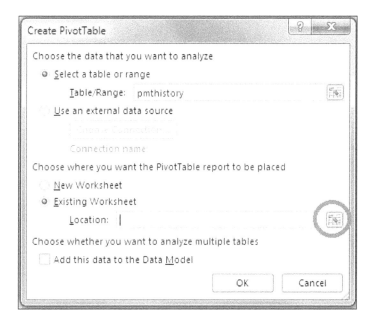

3. When the dialog box appears, select the **report** tab and click on cell **A1**, as shown in the following screenshot. After cell **A1** is selected, press the *Enter* key on your keyboard and then click on **OK** in the dialog box.

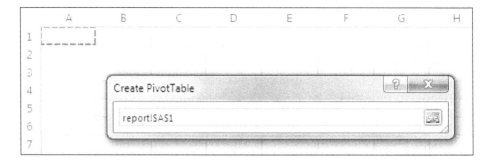

4. In the **PivotTable** wizard, choose the **userid** and **price** columns, as shown in the following screenshot. The only issue is that we want to take the sum and not the count of the **price** column. Let's change this in step 5.

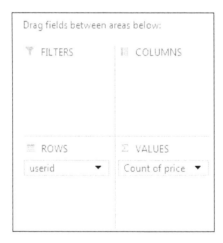

5. Click on the **Count of price** drop-down menu and select the **Value Field Settings...** option.

6. Choose **sum** and click on the **OK** button. You will now get results similar to the following screenshot:

You will also get a pivot table in cell **A1** that looks similar to the following screenshot. See the problem here? We would prefer to see the actual names of the properties instead of their IDs. Where can we find the names of the properties? Yes, in the **users** table. We can use another formula to bring in the property names, but we will make use of the data model in the following steps:

	A	B
1	**Row Labels**	**Sum of price**
2	1	9
3	2	12
4	3	92
5	50	#N/A
6	99	#N/A
7	**Grand Total**	**#N/A**

Data models

What are data models? They are just models, which you create, that allow you to combine data from multiple sources.

Why data models? In reality, you do not need to use data models at all. Filters, formulas, and pivot tables are sufficient for all your data needs. Data models, however, give you the ability to work with larger datasets than your typical Excel sheet can handle. They also allow you to combine data from multiple tables without using VLOOKUPS. The following example shows you how this can be done:

1. Select the **pmthistory** tab and then select any cell with data in it. Navigate to the **INSERT** tab and click on the **PivotTable** button, as we did in *Analyzing data* section of this chapter. Also, select the location where we want to place the table in cell **D1**. We will also need to check the **Add this data to the Data Model** option, as shown in the following screenshot. Finally, click on the **OK** button.

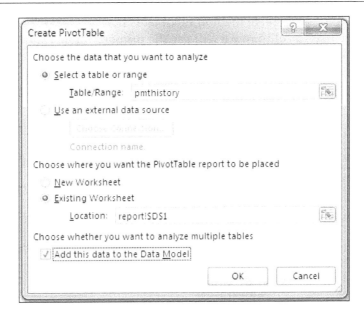

2. Click on the **ALL** tab, and you will be able to see all of your tables. This means that you now have access to all of the columns in any of the tables. You will soon see why this is so amazing and all thanks to Excel's data models.

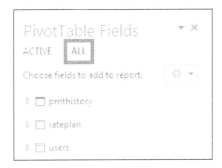

3. We are going to recreate the first pivot table that we made, but instead of using the **userid** column, we will use the **propertyname** column from the **users** table and the **price** column from the **pmyhistory** table, as shown in the following screenshot. Do you see an issue? All of the values are **137** and this is not correct. In other words, we need to tell Excel how each of the tables relate to each other.

4. Click one the **CREATE** button.

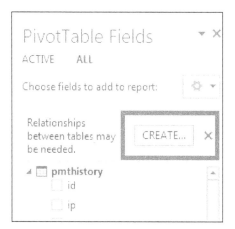

5. In the **Create Relationship** dialog box, fill in the values, as shown in the following screenshot, and click on the **OK** button. The **Related Table** and **Related Column** options are for the tables that have unique values. This table is usually referred to as a lookup table. Excel does a good job of letting you know if you place the tables in the wrong order, so you should not worry too much here.

For those familiar with SQL, we basically created an inner join that looks like this:

```
SELECT *
FROM pmthistory a
JOIN users b on (a.userid = b.id)
```

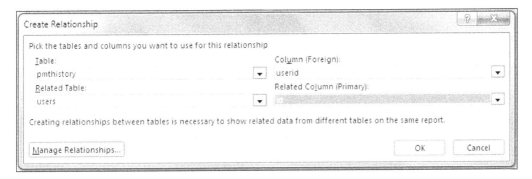

You will now get results similar to the following screenshot. We just created a pivot table that included data from two different tables. This is really an amazing feat for Excel! The tricky part was figuring out step 5, but after that it was a breeze.

D Row Labels	E Count of price
property1	9
property2	92
property3	12
(blank)	24
Grand Total	**137**

One last issue is that Excel does not allow us to sum up the **price** column. We can resolve this by cleaning up the data in the **price** column from the original **pmthistory** table.

6. Replace all **#N/A** with zeros, as shown in the following screenshot:

7/12/2014	1
7/13/2014	1
7/20/2014	0
7/20/2014	0
7/20/2014	0

7. Go to your pivot table in the **report** tab. Select your pivot table, and under the **ANALYZE** tab, click on the **Refresh** button.

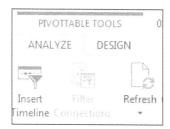

You can now change the **price** column to be the sum and not the count in the pivot table editor. You can also format the cells to **currency** and get results similar to the following screenshot. Were you able to do it? Good job!

D	E
Row Labels	**Sum of price**
property1	$ 9.00
property2	$ 92.00
property3	$ 12.00
(blank)	$ -
Grand Total	**$ 113.00**

If you said that Fast Forms made a total of $113 in 2014, then you are unfortunately incorrect. We did not consider whether the applications submitted were successful or not. Recall from the previous sections that Fast Forms will only charge their customers for successful applications. We'll go back to this issue in a later chapter.

Summary

I hope you enjoyed this chapter and all of the previous ones leading up to this point. By now, you should be very competent and able to understand the data analysis life cycle. We covered most of the stages except the presentation stage. This chapter focused on building your data preparation skills. It took us a while to get to the data models, but it was important to go through the previous steps so that you could appreciate this new functionality. There is a lot more that we could have done in this chapter, and I'm sure that we could create a book just on data models but we only had one chapter in this case. If you have one of the premium versions of Excel, there are a lot more tools that can be used in conjunction with data models, such as Power View, but I will let you discover this on your own. Being able to merge data from various sources and slice your data using data from various places is a skill that we practiced in this chapter. We were able to answer insightful questions about data by using data models and pivot tables. These are advanced topics and the more you practice, the better you will get. In the next chapter, we move up a gear and learn about the Excel Solver.

7

A Primer on Using the Excel Solver

My aim in this chapter is to introduce you to the famous Excel Solver. Together, we will start from activating the Excel add-in to solving the business problems you might encounter in your line of work. The Excel Solver will assume that you have some background in **linear programming**, thus making this an advanced topic. We will aim to concentrate on simple optimization problems and attempt to be as practical as possible. Where does this chapter fit into the data analysis life cycle? Well, the data analysis section, of course. This is the part that comes after you have prepared your data and you are ready for analysis. At this point, you should have a good understanding of your data and know what needs to be done with your data. In the past, I have used the Excel Solver to automate tedious and repetitive tasks. These tasks used to take several hours, but now they take under a minute. This was monumental for my department at that time and gave us the freedom to concentrate on other tasks. These are the kinds of results I want you to have after you soak in the knowledge this chapter has to offer. Are you ready?

Activating the Excel Solver

Excel does not have the Solver feature turned on by default, so we have to tell Excel to turn it on for us. Let's perform the following steps to activate the Excel Solver:

1.   Fire up Excel 2013 and create a new spreadsheet. Go to the **FILE** menu and select the **Options** button, as shown in the following screenshot:

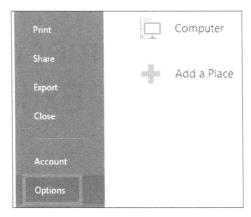

Figure 7.1

2.   In the **Excel Options** dialog box, select the **Add-Ins** option.

Figure 7.2

Notice that the **Solver Add-in** option is under the **Inactive Application Add-ins** menu option, as shown in the following screenshot:

Figure 7.3

3.   Click on the **Go...** button, which is at the bottom of the dialog box.

Figure 7.4

4.   In the **Add-Ins** dialog box, check the box labeled **Solver Add-in** and click on the **OK** button.

Figure 7.5

If you navigate to the **DATA** tab, you will have a new button labeled **Solver**, as shown in the following screenshot. Congratulations! You have activated the Excel Solver in just a few steps.

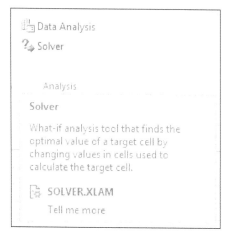

Figure 7.6

Modeling our linear programming problem

Let's take a look at the following problem carefully. We are going to formulate the pieces needed to solve a linear problem on paper and then use Excel to find the answer.

Problem: Imagine that you work for a company that sells baseball bats and you get the following request. The company wants to make a certain number of wooden bats and metal bats. The total number of bats that we want to make is 50 but we can make fewer if needed. We do have a requirement to make at least 25 bats. It costs the company $10 to make wooden bats and $20 to make metal bats. The total budget that we have to work with amounts to $1,000. We also have to make the bats quickly as we need to have them ready for sale in 48 hours or less. It takes 1 hour to make a wooden bat and 2 hours to make a metal bat. The company can sell the wooden bats at $15 each and the metal bats at $40 each. Your job is to find how many wooden and metal bats to make in order to maximize profits for the company.

Let's start by declaring our variables:

x = Wooden bat

y = Metal bat

Re-read the word problem, and let's start by writing down our constraints.

The following constraint says that the total number of wooden (x) and metal (y) bats can be any number less than or equal to 50:

- *x + y <= 50 bats*

The request also tells us that we have to make at least 25 bats:

- *x + y >= 25 bats*

Since we have a budget, we have to make sure that we do not exceed it:

- *10x + 20y <= 1000 dollars*

There is also a time limit of 48 hours that we have to take into consideration:

- *x + 2y <= 48 hours*

The most important piece to get correct is the objective function. If you read the word problem one more time, you can see that the whole purpose of the task is to maximize profits for the company. The following function is the function that we are trying to maximize while staying within the constraints we have already laid out:

- *MAX: 15x + 40y*

Now, we get to the fun part. We are now going to use the Excel Solver to find the answer to this problem. In the following steps, you will learn how to code this model into Excel and solve it using the Solver:

1. Make sure that you are on **Sheet1** of your workbook. In cell **A1**, type `Variables`, as shown in the following screenshot:

Figure 7.7

2. In cell **A2**, type `Wooden Bat (x)` and in cell **A3**, type `Metal Bat (y)`. Make sure that you apply **All Borders** to cells **A2** through **B3**, as shown in the following screenshot:

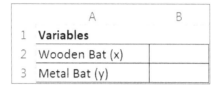

Figure 7.8

3. In cell **A5**, type `Constraints` and make the text bold. Under this heading, we are going to enter all of the equations we defined in the introduction of this section. We are going to start with the following constraint:

   ○ $x + y <= 50$ bats

How are we going to enter this equation into Excel? In cell **A6**, type `=B2+B3` and press the *Enter* button on your keyboard. Notice that cell **B2** represents **x** and cell **B3** represents **y**. Cells **B2** and **B3** represent the cells that are going to hold the optimal numbers that will generate the most revenue. These are the two cells that Excel will fill in for us. All that we are doing now is setting up the problem so that Excel can then do all the hard work and find an answer.

Figure 7.9

In cell **B6**, type `<=` and press the *Enter* button on your keyboard. Notice that the formula we created in cell **A6** gives us a value of zero. Make sure that you also get the same results, as shown in the following screenshot:

Figure 7.10

In cell **C6**, type `50`.

Figure 7.11

4. Let's give the following constraint a try. Can you figure it out?

    ◦   *x + y >= 25 bats*

How are we going to enter this equation into Excel? In cell **A7**, type =B2+B3 and press the *Enter* key on your keyboard. These are the same initial steps that we performed in the previous step.

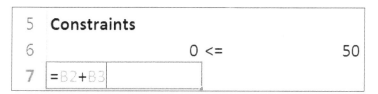

5	**Constraints**		
6		0 <=	50
7	=B2+B3		

Figure 7.12

In cell **B7**, type >= and press the *Enter* key on your keyboard. Make sure that you also get the same results, as shown here:

5	**Constraints**		
6		0 <=	50
7		0 >=	

Figure 7.13

In cell **C7**, type 25.

5	**Constraints**		
6		0 <=	50
7		0 >=	25

Figure 7.14

5. The next constraint will be entered as follows:

    ◦   *10x + 20y <= 1000 dollars*

In cell **A8**, type `=(10*B2)+(20*B3)` and press the *Enter* key on your keyboard, as shown in the following screenshot:

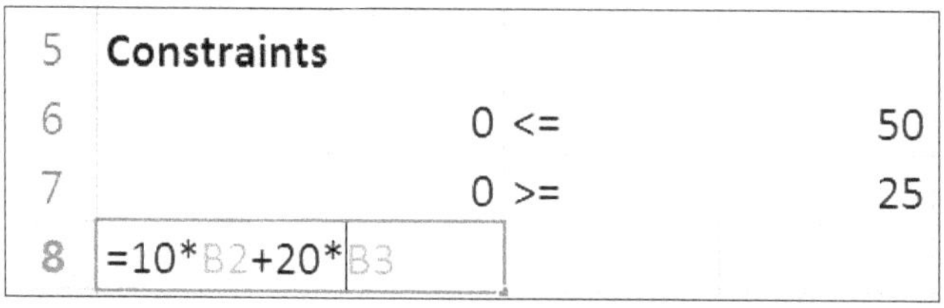

5	**Constraints**		
6		0 <=	50
7		0 >=	25
8	`=10*B2+20*B3`		

Figure 7.15

In cell **B8**, type `<=` and press the *Enter* button on your keyboard. In cell **C8**, type `1000`.

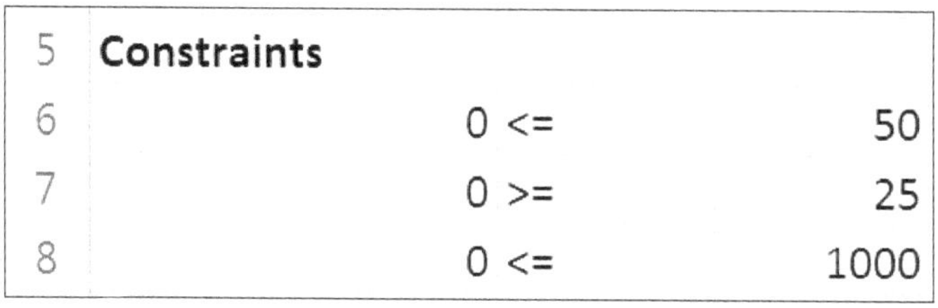

5	**Constraints**		
6		0 <=	50
7		0 >=	25
8		0 <=	1000

Figure 7.16

6. Let's complete the section by modeling one more constraint:

   ○ *x + 2y <= 48 hours*

In cell **A9**, type `=B2+2*B3` and press the *Enter* key on your keyboard.

5	**Constraints**		
6		0 <=	50
7		0 >=	25
8		0 <=	1000
9	`=B2+2*B3`		

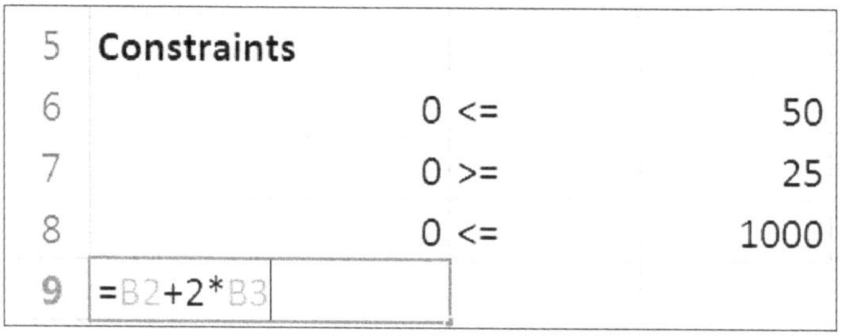

Figure 7.17

In cell **B9**, type <= and press the *Enter* key on your keyboard. In cell **C9**, type 48.

5	**Constraints**		
6		0 <=	50
7		0 >=	25
8		0 <=	1000
9		0 <=	48

Figure 7.18

I know that this was a bit tedious and time consuming, but the idea was to get you to type and gain experience. In essence, what we are doing here is modeling our problem in the language Excel understands. Now that we have all of our constraints completed, all that is left is to write our objective function. Again, I understand that I have thrown around a lot of "jargons", but this is an advanced chapter. I am assuming that you already know the math behind **linear programming**, and I am only going to show you the steps to model and solve a basic LP problem:

7.   In cell **A11**, type Objective, make the text bold, and add a border to cell **A12**.

11	**Objective**
12	

Figure 7.19

8.   In cell **A12**, type =15*B2+40*B3 and then press the *Enter* key on your keyboard.

11	**Objective**
12	=15*B2+40*B3

Figure 7.20

   ○   *48 <= 48*

You will now have a spreadsheet identical to the following screenshot. Notice that I added some borders to the **Constraint** section just to maintain consistency. It is not important to know how you can lay out the numbers and formulas, as long as you understand what is going on in the spreadsheet. Keep in mind that even though the constraints in column **C** are all constants, these cells can also contain formulas.

	A	B	C
1	**Variables**		
2	Wooden Bat (x)		
3	Metal Bat (y)		
4			
5	**Constraints**		
6	0	<=	50
7	0	>=	25
8	0	<=	1000
9	0	<=	48
10			
11	**Objective**		
12	0		

Figure 7.21

Using the Excel Solver

Before we start, let's review the problem we are trying to solve. Re-read the problem presented in the *Modeling our linear programming problem* section. We are given the task of maximizing the revenue with some constraints. We have to decide how many wooden bats and metal bats to produce to maximize profits. Why don't we just make as many metal bats as possible since they make the most profit? Well, we can certainly try this strategy. Using the spreadsheet that we built in the *Modeling our linear programming problem* section, we can type numbers in cells **B2** and **B3**. Cell **A12** will tell us how much revenue our educated guess brings us. The bigger the number you put in cells **B2** and **B3**, the more revenue you will accumulate. But remember that we cannot violate our constraints. For example, if we purchase zero wooden bats and 50 metal bats, we will violate the constraint in row 9. Do you see that? If we produced 50 metal bats, it would take us 100 hours to produce this many metal bats. We had a time limit of 48 hours, so this combination will not work.

Try a few more guesses and see whether you can come up with a combination that satisfies all of the constraints. How do you know when you have the best possible answer? Well yes, you can try every possible combination of wooden and metal bats and then pick the best option. Is there a better way? Yes! Excel will be more than happy to find the answer for you. The following series of steps will show you how to do this:

1. Open the file named 02 - Lesson.xlsx in the code files present for this chapter in the Chapter 07 folder. You will see something similar to *Figure 7.21* in the *Modeling our linear programming problem* section.

2. Select the **DATA** tab and click on the button named **Solver**.

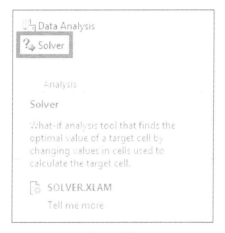

Figure 7.22

You will get the **Solver Parameters** dialog box, as shown in the following screenshot:

Figure 7.23

For the **Set Objective:** parameter, select cell **A12**. Make sure that the **To:** parameter is set to **Max** if it has not been selected by default. The objective function is the formula that we are trying to either maximize or minimize. We can also try to achieve a specific number, but in most cases, we are either trying to maximize or minimize something.

3. The **By Changing Variable Cells** parameter should be set to cells **B2** and **B3**. These are the cells that Excel will enter values for our solution. Make sure that the **Make Unconstrained Variables Non-Negative** checkbox is checked. This just means that Excel cannot use negative numbers for the final solution. In other words, it does not make sense to produce a negative amount of wooden or metal bats. In general, negative numbers don't make sense, but it just depends on the problem you are trying to solve. Make sure that the **Select a Solving Method** drop-down menu is set to **Simplex LP**. We are not going to discuss what algorithms are best suited to certain problems, as this is outside the scope of this book.

After completing steps 2 and 3, compare your screen with the following screenshot. Don't try to just type the cell references manually. Use the buttons with tiny red arrows to the right of each parameter to select your cells.

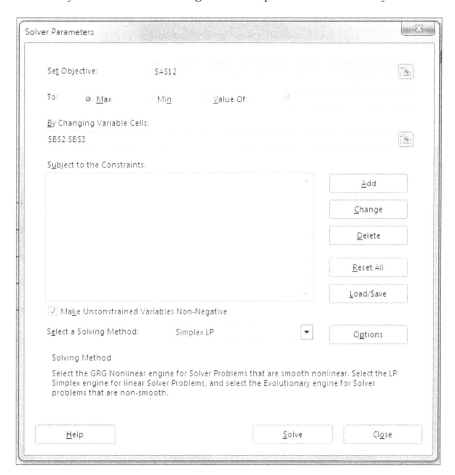

Figure 7.24

4. Our next task is to enter our constraints. Click on the **Add** button in the **Solver Parameters** dialog box. You will get the **Add Constraint** dialog box, as shown in the following screenshot:

Figure 7.25

5. Click on the **Cell Reference** button.

Figure 7.26

6. Select cell **A6** in the **Add Constraint** dialog box and press the *Enter* key on your keyboard.

Figure 7.27

7. Cell **B6** says <= and so does the **Add Constraint** dialog box, so no changes are needed here. Click on the **Constraint** button.

Figure 7.28

8. Select cell **C6** and press the *Enter* key on your keyboard. You will now have a dialog box similar to the following screenshot:

Figure 7.29

9. Click on the **OK** button in the **Add Constraint** dialog box.

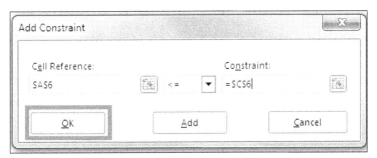

Figure 7.30

You will now see a newly added constraint in the **Solver Parameters** dialog box.

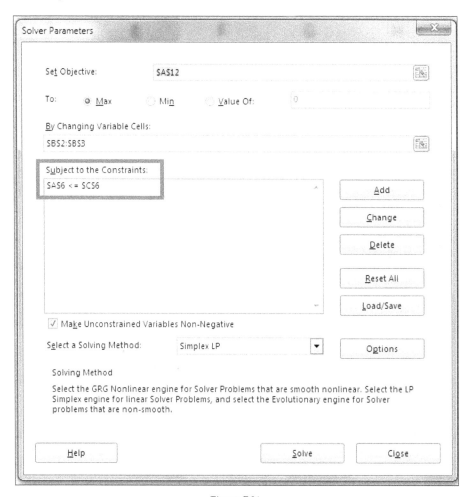

Figure 7.31

10. Click on the **Add** button to initiate adding another constraint. For the **Cell Reference** parameter, select cell **A7**, as shown in the following screenshot:

Figure 7.32

11. Select the **>=** inequality sign, as shown here:

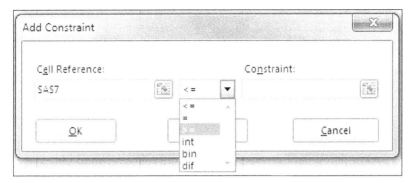

Figure 7.33

12. For the **Constraint** parameter, select cell **C7**. You will now have values that resemble the following screenshot:

Figure 7.34

After you click on the **OK** button in the **Add Constraint** dialog box, you will get the **Solver Parameters** dialog box.

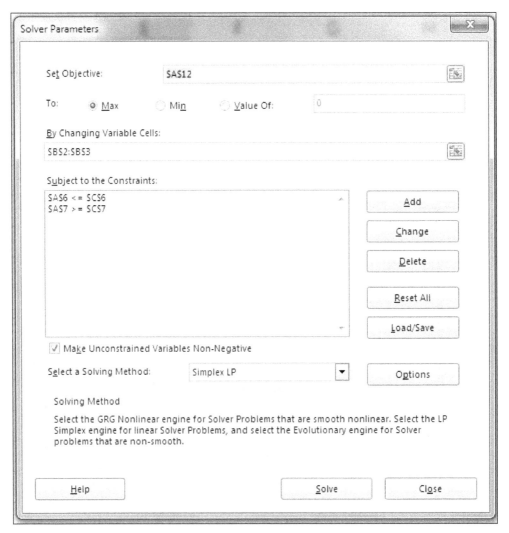

Figure 7.35

13. Using the knowledge that we learned in the previous steps, add the remaining two constraints. Take a look at the following screenshot for reference:

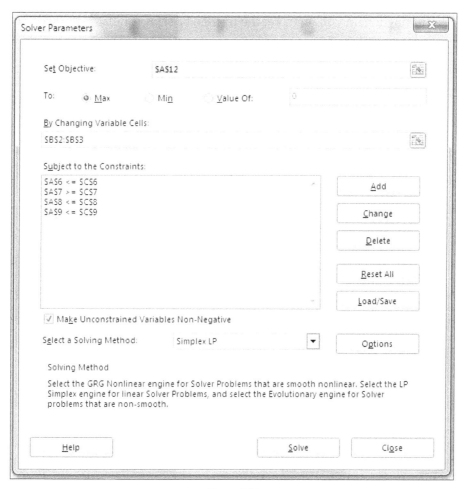

Figure 7.36

14. Now that you have modeled the problem in Excel, it is time to let Excel do the heavy lifting. Click on the **Solve** button in the **Solver Parameters** dialog box. You will get a new dialog box named **Solver Results**, as shown in the following screenshot. Click on the **OK** button to continue. The **Reports** section will help you interpret the results, but this is outside the scope of this book.

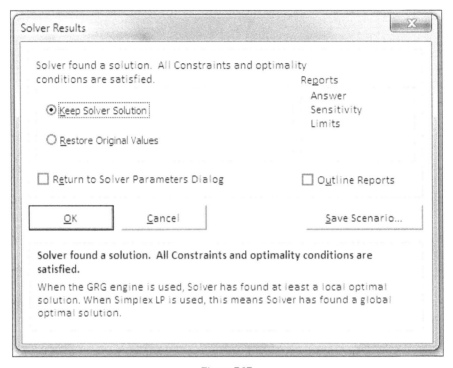

Figure 7.37

Also, notice that Excel has added the solution to cells **B2** and **B3**.

Variables	
Wooden Bat (x)	2
Metal Bat (y)	23

Figure 7.38

Excel says that the optimal solution produces **2** wooden bats and **23** metal bats. This is the combination that will yield the largest profits while satisfying all of the constraints. We are predicting that if we produce **2** wooden bats and **23** metal bats, we will make $950 profit in total revenue from the sale of the bats. Let's go through each of the constraints and see whether the solution makes sense.

	A	B	C
1	**Variables**		
2	Wooden Bat (x)	2	
3	Metal Bat (y)	23	
4			
5	**Constraints**		
6		25 <=	50
7		25 >=	25
8		480 <=	1000
9		48 <=	48
10			
11	**Objective**		
12		950	

Figure 7.39

We recommend you produce 25 bats in total, and the original constraint stated that we wanted to produce a maximum of 50 bats:

- *25 <= 50*

We recommend you produce 25 bats in total, and the original constraint stated that we wanted to produce at least 25 bats:

- *25 >= 25*

We recommend you spend a total of $480, and the original constraint stated that our total budget was restricted to $1,000:

- *480 <= 1000*

We recommend you spend 48 hours producing bats, and the original constraint stated that we wanted to spend a maximum of 48 hours producing bats:

- *48 <= 48*

What is great about this model is that we can answer "what if?" questions. Let's say that we are able to produce metal bats at $15 per bat instead of $20 per bat. Would your answer change? Yes, it would! All we have to do is modify our constraint in cell **A8** and rerun the Solver. What if we had 72 hours to produce our bats instead of 48 hours? We would then just modify cell **C9** and rerun the solver. See the power of Excel and see the power you now have. You have just equipped yourself with a spreadsheet that can adjust to dozens of different scenarios and still come up with the best answer.

If you have made it to this point, pat yourself on the back. Most Excel developers do not understand the Solver or how to use it, and those folks are now in the rear view mirror. This chapter has shown you the advanced uses of Excel that can help you solve problems your company has not been able to wrap their heads around. You can also use the Solver to simply automate decisions that are currently being done manually. For example, selling inventory can be turned into a linear programming problem very easily. The objective function is just maximizing the profit and the constraints can just be the number of inventory items that are available.

Summary

This chapter can be very challenging for those who have not heard of the term linear programming. For those who enjoy this subject, other terms such as machine learning and data mining will make them smile. The good news is that professionals with these skills like yourself are very sought after and get compensated generously. After reading this chapter, you have learned how to model a linear programming problem and tell Excel to solve it for you. We will continue attaining advanced Excel skills and get introduced to VBA, Excel's scripting language.

8
Learning VBA – Excel's Scripting Language

This chapter is either going to push you toward becoming a developer or push you to stay on the analysis side of the house. VBA is a simple programming language and this means that you have to write code. Now, do not be discouraged as you have already been writing little bits of code. When did I write the code? Remember those formulas that we have been "coding" in the previous chapters. You were writing the code and this is the reason why you should not be afraid of Excel's VBA. Excel's scripting language is going to give you the power to automate repetitive tasks and get the work done faster using macros. You will now have the power to give Excel instructions and offload some of your data analysis steps to Excel. We are going to start by defining some terms, writing the VBA code, and finally, putting it to use.

What is VBA?

VBA stands for **Visual Basic for Applications** and was primarily designed to give you the ability to extend Excel's features. By default, Excel already has a vast amount of tools to help you in the data analysis life cycle. We have already seen a small sample in the previous chapters of this book. The problem of performing repetitive tasks becomes very apparent when you are analyzing data. For example, you may be removing leading spaces constantly in your daily work. So, instead of creating formulas, you can create and write some VBA code and bind it to a keyboard shortcut. The next time you need to remove a leading space from a cell, you can just call the VBA code you wrote and it is instantly done. If it is not clear how VBA can help you, that is okay, as you can continue educating yourself and going through some examples, and then everything will make more sense.

What is a macro?

An Excel macro is a set of instructions that can be run over and over again. These instructions are written in VBA, thus a macro is created by writing the VBA code. You can also create a macro without writing any VBA code, but getting some exposure to a macro will be beneficial to you.

Opening the VBA Editor

The following steps will show you how to activate the **Developer** menu, which you will need to create your VBA code:

1. Fire up Excel 2013 and create a new spreadsheet. Go to the **FILE** menu and select the **Options** button, as shown in the following screenshot:

2. In the **Excel Options** dialog box, select the **Customize Ribbon** option.

3. On the right-hand side of the **Excel Options** dialog box, check the **Developer** checkbox, as shown in the following screenshot. Then, click on the **OK** button to apply the changes.

You will now see that the **DEVELOPER** menu has been added to the ribbon.

4. Select the **DEVELOPER** tab and click on the **Visual Basic** button.

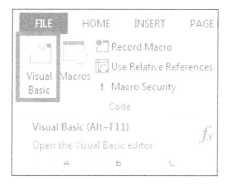

 You do not need to activate the **DEVELOPER** tab. You simply need to press the *ALT + F11* keys on your keyboard to open the VBA Editor.

Excel will open a new window, which is named Microsoft Visual Basic for Applications - Book1, and will have a project pane similar to the following screenshot:

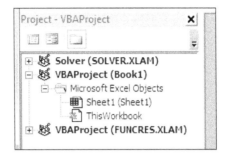

Congratulations! You are now ready to begin coding and ready to enter a new realm of the Excel world. Let's get started!

Your very first "Hello World" VBA script

We are going to start with a very simple script and then get into coding some useful VBA code. To start with, we are simply going to create a macro that displays a message box when it runs. These sections will help you visualize the steps needed to code, create, and deploy your macros.

1. Press the *ALT + F11* keys to open the VBA editor in case you closed this window after our last section.

2. Click on the **Insert** menu and select the **Module** option, as shown in the following screenshot. You need to create a module before you can begin writing any code. In other words, modules hold the VBA code.

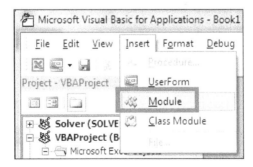

You will get a new window and have an object explorer that looks similar to the following screenshot. You can change the name of **Module1**, but for this section, we are going to keep the default name.

3. Type the following code into the module:

```
Sub Hello_World()

    ' My first VBA sub procedure
    MsgBox ("Hello World")

End Sub
```

Can you explain this code to me?

On line one, we have the `Sub Hello_World()` code. We start all of our sub procedures or functions with the word `Sub` followed by the name of the function. In this example, we called our function `Hello_World`. We then complete it with a set of parentheses. The next line is what is normally referred to as a comment. A comment is simply the text we type that is ignored by Excel. Comments are usually used to document your code, and I highly encourage you to comment your code all of the time. In VBA, we use an apostrophe to let Excel know that we are about to write a comment. Also, note that the text gets highlighted in green. The next line starts with a built-in function called `MsgBox`, which simply means a message box. The message we want to display is included in parentheses and double quotes. We end all of our functions with the `End Sub` code. Let's now try to run the `Hello_World` macro and see what it actually does.

4. Toggle back to your Excel file by pressing the *ALT + F11 keys*. Press the *ALT + F8* keys to initiate the **Macro** window that will show you all of the available macros, as shown in the following screenshot. We can see that the only available macro we have is the one we just created called **Hello_World**.

5. To run the macro, you can simply select the **Hello_World** macro and press the *Enter* key on your keyboard. You can also run the macro by selecting it and clicking on the **Run** button. After running the macro, you will get a dialog box similar to the one in the following screenshot. Click on the **OK** button to remove the message box.

Declaring variables

In this section, we will create another version of the `Hello_World` function that uses variables. As your VBA scripts get more and more complex, you can eventually start to incorporate variables into your code.

1. Create a second sub procedure right below `Hello_World` and name it `Hello_World2`, as shown in the following screenshot:

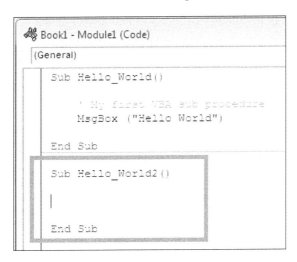

2. Enter the following code in `Hello World2`. We have declared a variable named `Year` and another one named `Text`. The `Year` variable is of `Integer` type, which means that this variable can hold numeric data. The variable named `Text` is of `String` type, which means that this variable can hold text data:

```
' Declare Variables
Dim Year As Integer
Dim Text As String
```

```
Sub Hello_World2()

    ' Declare Variables
    Dim Year As Integer
    Dim Text As String

End Sub
```

3. To actually assign values to these two variables, type the following code, as shown in the following screenshot. As expected, we assigned a numeric value to `Year` and assigned an alpha character to the variable named `Text`:

```
' Set Variables
Year = 2015
Text = "Hello World! It is"
```

```
Sub Hello_World2()

    ' Declare Variables
    Dim Year As Integer
    Dim Text As String

    ' Set Variables
    Year = 2015
    Text = "Hello World! It is"

End Sub
```

4. Let's now create a message box that includes both of these variables. Refer to the following screenshot for reference. As you can see, our goal here is to create a message that says **Hello World! It is 2015**. Note that we use the plus (**+**) sign to combine both the variables:

```
MsgBox (Text + Year)
```

```
Sub Hello_World2()

    ' Declare Variables
    Dim Year As Integer
    Dim Text As String

    ' Set Variables
    Year = 2015
    Text = "Hello World! It is"

    ' Print Message
    MsgBox (Text + Year)

End Sub
```

5. Press the *Alt + F11* keys to switch over to the Excel file. Press the *Alt + F8* keys, choose **Hello_World2**, and run the macro. You will get an error message similar to the following screenshot. Oh no! What does this mean? This means that Excel has encountered an error while running the macro.

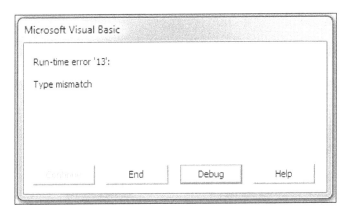

6. Click on the **Debug** button in the **Microsoft Visual Basic** dialog box to find out exactly where our error is located. Excel will then proceed to highlight the code that is causing the error, as shown in the following screenshot. Can you figure out what the issue is?

```
Sub Hello_World2()

    ' Declare Variables
    Dim Year As Integer
    Dim Text As String

    ' Set Variables
    Year = 2015
    Text = "Hello World! It is"

    ' Print Message
    MsgBox (Text + Year)

End Sub
```

The error message we got from step 5 says **Type mismatch** and this means that Excel does not like you to combine the Year and Text variables. Remember that the Year variable was of Integer type and the Text variable was of String type. In order to combine them, as we tried to do so, both the variables must be of the same type. We can accomplish this by converting the Year variable from Integer type to String type. How can we do this? Step 7 will show you how to do this.

7. Before we proceed, make sure that you shut down the macro. Since it is still running, we need to stop the macro in order to edit the code. To do this, simply click on the **Reset** button, as shown in the following screenshot:

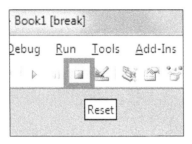

8. To convert or cast the Year variable, modify your code to match the following screenshot:

```
Sub Hello_World2()

    ' Declare Variables
    Dim Year As Integer
    Dim Text As String

    ' Set Variables
    Year = 2015
    Text = "Hello World! It is"

    ' Print Message
    MsgBox (Text + Str(Year))

End Sub
```

9. Now, try to run the **Hello_World2** macro after you make the changes. You will not get any error message but will see a message box similar to this:

Congratulations! You have just written and debugged the VBA code. You now know how to create sub procedures and use variables. This is monumental in your journey to becoming a proficient Excel developer. Good job!

Conditional statements

Conditional statements are a big part of many programming languages. They allow you to react to various situations and give your programs the flexibility they need. In this section, we will create a sub procedure that uses a user input to decide what kind of output to show the end user.

Create a new function called Question and enter the following code:

```
Sub Question()

    ' Declare Variables
    Dim num As Integer

    ' Ask user a question
    num = InputBox("How many apples do you want to buy?",
      "Checkout")

    ' Make sure user does not pick a value greater than 20
    ' Make sure user does not pick a negative
    If num < 0 Or num > 20 Then

        ' Print Message
        MsgBox ("Please select a postive number or a value less
          than 21.")
```

```
      Else

          ' Print Message
          MsgBox ("You want to buy" + Str(num) + " apples.")

      End If
```

```
Sub Question()

    ' Declare Variables
    Dim num As Integer

    ' Ask user a question
    num = InputBox("How many apples do you want to buy?", "Checkout")

    ' Make sure user does not pick a value grater than 20
    ' Make sure user does not pick a negative
    If num < 0 Or num > 20 Then

        ' Print Message
        MsgBox ("Please select a postive number or a value less than 21.")

    Else

        ' Print Message
        MsgBox ("You want to buy" + Str(num) + " apples.")

    End If

End Sub
```

This macro asks the user for a number and then, based on what the user enters, the macro will return a message. You are already familiar with variables and the MsgBox function, so we will go through these lines of code. Notice that the InputBox function has two parameters. The first one is the question we want to ask the end user. The second one is optional and it is the title of the InputBox function. When the end user enters a number, that number is saved in our variable named num.

The conditional statement starts with the word If followed by a condition that is either true or false. If it is true, it will execute the code after the word Then. If it is false, it will execute the code after the word Else. Conditional statements end with End If. Did this make sense?

Loops

If you ever need to repeat certain parts of your code, then you will most likely be using loops to accomplish this task. We will create a simple function that shows you how loops are written in VBA. By now, you should be more comfortable with VBA and hopefully enjoy it.

Create a new sub procedure called `Loopy` and enter the following code, as shown in the following screenshot:

```
Sub Loopy()

    ' Declare Variables
    Dim num As Integer
    Dim counter As Integer

    ' Initialize variables
    counter = 0

    ' Ask user a question
    num = InputBox("How many times to loop?", "Loopy")

    ' Loop while the value of counter is less than num
    Do While counter < num

        ' Print Message
        MsgBox ("Looping...")

        ' Increment counter
        counter = counter + 1

    Loop

End Sub
```

To initiate a loop, start with `Do While` followed by a condition that is true or false. The `While` loop will end with the word `Loop`. All of the code that is in between will be executed as long as the `counter < num` condition is true. Run the macro and try it out for yourself!

Creating macros without any code

Is it possible to create a macro without writing any code? Yes! Excel gives you the ability to record steps you create and save them as the VBA code that can be reused. Let's take an example from *Chapter 3, How to Clean Texts, Numbers, and Dates* and create a macro:

1. Go back to Excel by pressing the *Alt + F11* keys. Enter the following information in column **A**:

    Name

    david Rojas

    Bill Fergus

    Mary blue

    BOB BOBBY

    MikE HoPe

	A
1	**Name**
2	david Rojas
3	Bill Fergus
4	Mary blue
5	BOB BOBBY
6	MikE HoPe

What we want to do next is simple; make sure that the data is capitalized in a consistent manner. We have already learned that in order to do this, we will need to use the function called `Proper`. Let's record these steps and create a macro. Just follow the next steps.

2. Select the **VIEW** tab, click on the **Macros** drop-down menu, and select the **Record Macro** option, as shown in the following screenshot:

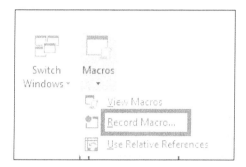

You will get a dialog box named **Record Macro**. We will leave all of the default values the same and click on the **OK** button.

3. Every single key stroke that you perform will be recorded, so do exactly as I say. Right-click on column **B** and select the **Insert** option, as shown in the following screenshot:

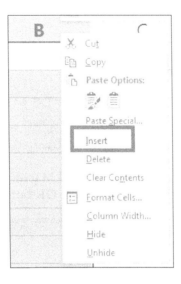

4. In cell **B1**, type Fixed, and in cell **B2**, type =proper(and select cell **A2**, as shown in the following screenshot. Make sure that you close the parentheses and press the *Enter* key on your keyboard.

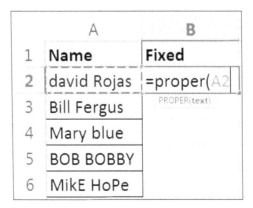

5. Go back to the **Macros** drop-down menu and select **Stop Recording**.

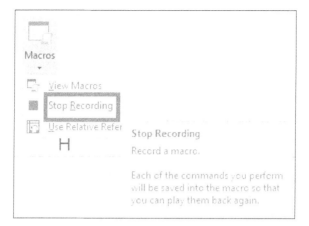

That's it! You have just created a macro. So, where is the macro located? Press the *ALT + F11* keys to find this out.

6. Double-click on the **Module2** object to see the code Excel has created for us.

The code you get back will look identical to the following screenshot:

```
Sub Macro1()
'
' Macro1 Macro
'

'
    Columns("B:B").Select
    Selection.Insert Shift:=xlToRight, CopyOrigin:=xlFormatFromLeftOrAbove
    Range("B1").Select
    ActiveCell.FormulaR1C1 = "Fixed"
    Range("B2").Select
    ActiveCell.FormulaR1C1 = "=PROPER(RC[-1])"
    Range("B3").Select
End Sub
```

As you can see, Excel was able to record every single action you took. The great news is that you can reuse this macro over and over again. Let's give it a try.

7. Go back to Excel by pressing the *ALT + F11* keys. Delete all of the contents of column **B**. Press the *ALT + F8* keys and run the macro named **Macro1**, as shown in the following screenshot. Wow! As you can see, Excel was able to fill in cells **B1** and **B2** automatically. If you change your data in column **A**, this macro will still work. This is incredible; this is Excel at its best!

> You can learn a lot of VBA code by just recording macros and studying the code Excel generates for us.

Can we create a macro that does even more? Can we create a macro that will clean not only the first cell but all of our cells? Yes! We can use the code from **Macro1** and tweak it so that it can work for any number of rows:

Create a new function, name it `Proper`, and enter the following code:

```
' Highlight Column B
Columns("B:B").Select

' Insert a column in between Columns A and B
Selection.Insert Shift:=xlToRight, CopyOrigin:=xlFormatFromLeftOr
Above

' Select cell B1
Range("B1").Select

' Label the column
ActiveCell.FormulaR1C1 = "Fixed"

' Select cell A2
Range("A2").Select

' Variable to keep track of active cell
FirstItem = ActiveCell.Text

' Variable that controls cell offset
Offsetcount = 1

' Loop until we run out of cells to clean
Do While ActiveCell.Text <> ""

    ' Add the proper formula to the cell one column to the right
    ActiveCell.Offset(0, Offsetcount).FormulaR1C1 =
"=PROPER(RC[-1])"
```

```
' Select the next cell we want to clean
FirstItem = ActiveCell.Offset(Offsetcount, 0).Select

Loop
```

```
Sub Proper()

    ' Highlight Column B
    Columns("B:B").Select

    ' Insert a column in between Columns A and B
    Selection.Insert Shift:=xlToRight, CopyOrigin:=xlFormatFromLeftOrAbove

    ' Select cell B1
    Range("B1").Select

    ' Label the column
    ActiveCell.FormulaR1C1 = "Fixed"

    ' Select cell A2
    Range("A2").Select

    ' Variable to keep track of active cell
    FirstItem = ActiveCell.Text

    ' Variable that controls cell offset
    Offsetcount = 1

    ' Loop until we run out of cells to clean
    Do While ActiveCell.Text <> ""

        ' Add the proper formula to the cell one column to the right
        ActiveCell.Offset(0, Offsetcount).FormulaR1C1 = "=PROPER(RC[-1])"

        ' Select the next cell we want to clean
        FirstItem = ActiveCell.Offset(Offsetcount, 0).Select

    Loop

End Sub
```

Let's go through the code line by line so that we can understand what we are doing here. Remember that the goal is to apply the `Proper` function to each cell in column **B**, as long as there is data in column **A**:

```
Columns("B:B").Select
```

All this code does is that it selects the entire column **B**. You can also use this code to select a range of cells or just one cell at a time:

```
Selection.Insert Shift:=xlToRight, CopyOrigin:=xlFormatFromLeftOr
Above
```

With column **B** selected, right-click, and insert a column between column **A** and column **B**. I know that this code is pretty confusing but all it does is that it inserts a new column:

```
Range("B1").Select
```

`Range` is another way to select specific cells, and it is very similar to *columns*. For our code in this function, they will behave identically, but there might be some differences in other situations. This code merely says to select cell **B1**. We select cell **B1** to add some text to it:

```
ActiveCell.FormulaR1C1 = "Fixed"
```

`ActiveCell` refers to the cell that is *active*. In our case, the active cell is **B1**, as the last piece of code says to select cell **B1**. The rest of the code just says to apply the following formula or text to that specific cell. We just added some text to the active cell, which in our case is cell **B1**:

```
Range("A2").Select
```

Nothing new here; we are just selecting cell **A2**. This is going to be the first cell that we are going to clean:

```
FirstItem = ActiveCell.Text
```

Notice that I did not declare the `FirstItem` variable. VBA does not require you to declare variables using the `Dim` method but this is not recommended. I only did this to show you that you don't have to declare a variable to use it but note that this is not ideal. In any case, we set this variable to be the currently active cell:

```
Offsetcount = 1
```

Yes, another undeclared variable. We use the `offsetcount` variable to hold the number of rows or columns to shift our cells. This will make sense as we will continue to review the rest of the code:

```
Do While ActiveCell.Text <> ""
```

Here is the start of the loop. It says to continue to loop as long as the active cell is not empty. What is our current active cell? Yes, it is **A2**. The rest of the code will change the active code to **A3**, then **A4**, and so on until the active cell has no data in it:

```
ActiveCell.Offset(0, Offsetcount).FormulaR1C1 = "=PROPER(RC[-1])"
```

This piece of code gets the active cell, moves one column to the right, and applies the Proper formula to the corresponding cell. The offset property has two parameters. The first one represents the rows and the second one represents the columns. Notice that RC[-1] represents the cell value of the previous column. In our case, the active cell is **A2** and when we shift it one to the right, we get to cell **B2**. It is in **B2** where we will apply the proper function. Pretty neat:

```
FirstItem = ActiveCell.Offset(Offsetcount, 0).Select
```

Since we are done with the current row, we move on to the next row. In our case, we started with column **A2** and added a formula to cell **B2**. We now will need to go from cell **A2** to cell **A3** and apply a function to cell **B3**. This code offsets or moves one row down from the currently active cell:

```
Loop
```

We continue to move down one row in column **A** until the active cell we are in is empty. This means that column **A** can have 5 or 5,000 records and our macro will go through each of them. This is pretty amazing! We just created a macro that will consistently capitalize the text and it does not matter how much data you have. The only constraint that we have is that the cells we want to consistently capitalize have to be in column **A**. Can you figure out how we can change the code so that we are not restricted to having our data in column **A**? Challenges like these will be the beginning of your programming journey. I love Excel!

Saving macro-powered spreadsheets

Excel will not let you save your file as a .xls file or a .xlsx file and will ask you to save this file using another type of extension. You need to save your workbook using the file type named Excel Macro-enabled workbook, as shown in the following screenshot:

File name:	Macros.xlsm
Save as type:	Excel Macro-Enabled Workbook (*.xlsm)
Authors:	david

Summary

We covered what VBA is and what a macro is all the way to creating sophisticated scripts to automate tasks. You learned about variables, data types, conditional statements, and loops. This alone will carry you very far in your programming journey. These concepts are very similar in many programming languages such as SQL, Python, and JavaScript. You got comfortable with the VBA Editor and got plenty of examples to create your very own Excel macros. We concluded the chapter with a very practical example of how you can leverage macros in your data preparation stage of the data analysis life cycle. From here, we will continue with the data presentation stage. In the next chapter, we will learn how to build effective charts to tell your very own data stories.

9

How to Build and Style Your Charts

Visually representing your data can arguably be called an art. Going from data to visualization, or "viz" for short, can actually be a lot of work. Just think about it; we have to first get the data, prepare it, analyze it, and then, we can finally try to chart it. Does this ring a bell? Yes, this is the data analysis life cycle we have been talking about over and over in this book. Now, my last statement does not mean that the only time you build a chart is at the end. Early in your exploratory phase, plotting your data can be very valuable in getting to know what you are working with. In this chapter, we are going to explore many of Excel's charting features and get you started with building vibrant visualizations. We will start with the quick and dirty charting options and then meticulously tweak our charts so that they convey the story you are trying to get across. We will not be going through every chart type and will only concentrate on some of the most common ones you will find in practice.

What types of charts go with what type of data?

- **Bar chart (column chart)**: This chart is used to make comparisons. The y axis is usually numeric and the x axis is categorical.

- **Line chart (time series chart)**: This chart is used to show trends over time. The y axis is usually numeric and the x axis is commonly composed of dates (categorical).

- **Pie chart**: This chart has traditionally been used to show percentages, but I personally try never to use this chart type. I feel that representing your data in a bar chart is a better option as it is much easier to see the differences between bars versus pie slices. This is especially true as the number of pie slices increase.

- **Scatter chart**: This chart is used to spot possible correlations/relationships between two unrelated sets of numerical data. For example, stock data has numerical values associated with dates. You should use a line chart when comparing data for two different stock symbols over time. The key is that they share a categorical axis and date axis. Data, such as precipitation versus temperature, does not share a categorical axis, thus a scatter chart is appropriate in this situation.

Quick analysis charts

Apart from the line chart, the bar chart is one of the most popular and useful charts you need to have in your tool belt. We will start by creating some data and then visualize it using Excel's **Quick Analysis** feature that is available in the 2013 version:

1. Fire up Excel 2013 and create a new spreadsheet. Manually enter the following data, as shown in the following screenshot:

	A	B
1	Date	Amount
2	1/1/2010	5
3	1/1/2011	100
4	1/1/2012	250
5	1/1/2013	500
6	1/1/2014	1500
7	1/1/2015	325

Figure 9.1

2. Highlight cells **A1** through **B7** and you will see a button appear in the bottom-right corner of your data, as shown in the following screenshot:

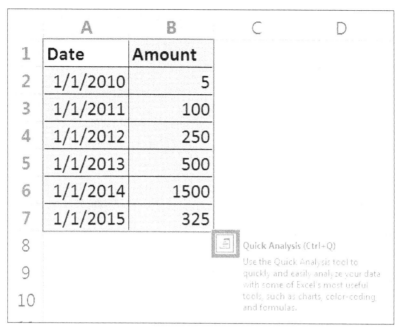

Figure 9.2

3. Click on the **Quick Analysis** button and select the **CHARTS** option.

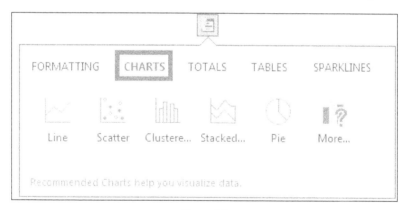

Figure 9.3

4. Hover over each of the different chart types and Excel will render the chosen chart type using your data. Pretty neat! Since we want to create a bar chart, click on the **Cluster...** option, and you will now have a chart that looks similar to the following screenshot:

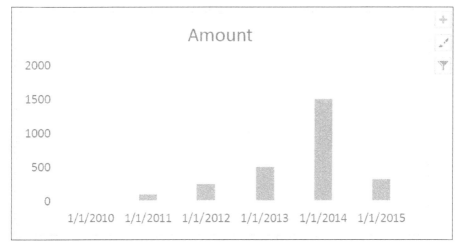

Figure 9.4

Let's pause here for a second and marvel at what just happened. All we did was highlight our data, clicked on a few menus, and, voila, we have a bar chart. Not only that, we could have also decided to generate a line chart and a stacked area chart. All of this with very little effort on our part. From this simple chart, we can see that the year 2014 had the greatest value and that most of the data is below 500. There is an issue with the year 2010. Can you see it? Yes, from the chart, it seems that the value for 2010 is zero, but we know from our data that this is not the case. Our data was also increasing over time until 2014, but that trend stopped in the year 2015. Note that I did not provide you with any context. Is this data sales data or the number of defects per year? Why do we only have the yearly data? This is the kind of information you need to obtain in the data gathering stage.

5. Select the bar chart we just created and press the *Delete* key on your keyboard. Repeat the previous steps, but instead of creating a bar chart, let's create a line chart, as shown here:

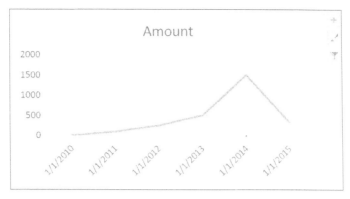

Figure 9.5

The line chart tells us about the similar information of the bar chart. The important dates are between 2013 and 2015. The peak of the chart occurs in the year 2014 and there is very little activity in the year 2010. Notice that the line chart makes us wonder whether the value for the year is very small or zero. The bar chart makes it pretty clear that the value present in the year 2010 is zero, but we know that this is not correct. Which of these charts would you choose to represent the data we created? I would include the raw data along with the chart so that we make sure that we are not misleading anyone interpreting our chart.

Charting options

In this chapter, we will go through various charting options Excel has to offer. Pay close attention as this section will help you polish your charts and make them look exactly how you need them to look. The previous section was not meant to create *perfect* looking charts but to quickly create a chart to gather insights about your data. This section assumes that you are in the presentation stage of the data analysis life cycle, and your goal is to create the best chart to convey a particular message to your audience. The following steps will show you how to create a chart that represents the number of defects that occurred over time for an imaginary company.

1. Select and delete the line chart we just finished creating. Rebuild the bar chart and click on the chart title.

Figure 9.6

This is the title of your chart and it is currently labeled as **Amount**. Excel used the name of the column and placed it in the title section as the default value. Let's change it to **Factory Defects**.

Figure 9.7

 You can make your chart title dynamic by adding a formula to the chart title label. Make sure that you first click on the text and type, for example =Sheet1!B2 in the formula bar.

2. Double-click on the *y* axis, as shown in the following screenshot. We are going to format the data so that the chart shows commas for figures in thousands.

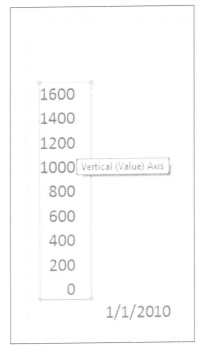

Figure 9.8

3. On the menu to the right called **Format Axis**, select the **Axis Options** button.

Figure 9.9

4. Expand the **NUMBER** menu, change the **Category** option from **General** to **Number**, and finally, change the **Decimal Places** from **2** to **0**.

Figure 9.10

If we go back to the chart, we will see that the y axis figures have now been formatted to show a comma, as shown in the following screenshot:

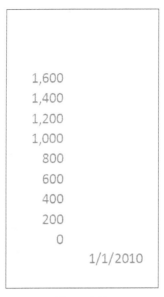

Figure 9.11

5. Notice that the dates in the x axis are all on the first of the month. We can make this chart a little cleaner and more readable if we only show the year. Showing the month and day might add value to your visualization, but in this example, we can say that just showing the year is sufficient. Select the x axis, as shown here:

Figure 9.12

6. Expand the **NUMBER** menu, change the **Format Code** option from **m/d/yyyy** to **yyyy**, and click on the **Add** button. Do not change anything under the **Type** option, as this will be adjusted by Excel automatically after you click on the **Add** button.

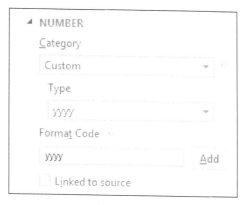

Figure 9.13

Your chart will now look like the one in the following screenshot. If you compare this chart to *Figure 9.4* of the *Quick analysis charts* section, you will see that the following screenshot is simpler and easier to understand.

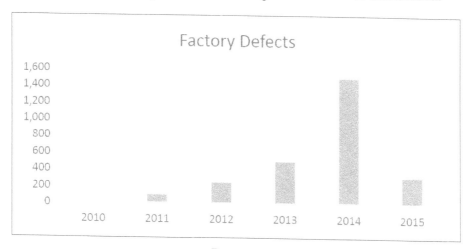

Figure 9.14

7. Click on any of the blue bars, select the **Fill & Line** option, expand the **FILL** menu, and change the **Color** from blue to orange.

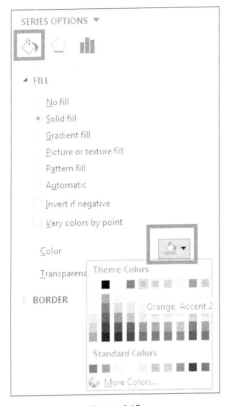

Figure 9.15

The color of the bars will now look like that of those in the following screenshot:

Figure 9.16

Chart elements

Excel 2013 gives you the ability to quickly change and modify different chart elements, such as the legend or chart title, with little effort. The following steps will guide you through the process:

1. Select the **Factory Defects** chart we have been working with. You will notice a plus sign on the right-hand side of the chart, as shown in the following screenshot. Click on the **+** sign button to activate the menu.

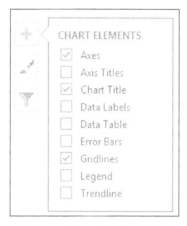

Figure 9.17

> The elements that have a check mark next to them are the ones that we already have in our chart. The **Axes** represents the dates and amount values. The **Chart Title** represents the **Factory Defects** label we have chosen for our chart. The **Gridlines** are the horizontal lines we see in the middle of our chart.

2. When you hover over all of the unchecked chart elements, you will see that the chart adds these elements to itself. Note that unless you add a check mark to the element, the chart element will not be added to your visualization.

Chart styles

You can also change the look and feel of your charts rather quickly. Excel gives you many options to customize your charts in a variety of styles.

Select the **Chart Styles** button. You will notice that there is a **STYLE** tab and a **COLOR** tab that allow you to customize your charts. Hover over several of the options and see whether you can find one that looks good to you.

Figure 9.18

Chart filters

Excel 2013 allows you to filter your data and only chart a slice of your data. The following steps will show you how to plot the chart using only the years 2014 and 2015:

Select the **Chart Filters** button, under the **CATEGORIES** section, click on the **(Select All)** option, and check the 2014 and 2015 boxes, as shown in the following screenshot. Make sure that you click on the **Apply** button to apply the changes.

Figure 9.19

Your chart will look like the one in the following screenshot. You can see that the chart only shows us the data points from the years 2014 and 2015. This means that you can customize your chart not only aesthetically, but you can also have a say on the data you want to show your audience.

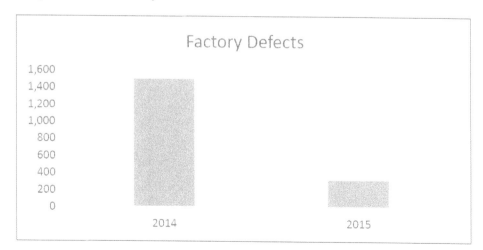

Figure 9.20

Additional design options

Excel also gives us the ability to change the layout of our charts. You can call them prebuilt templates that Excel prepares for us that we can choose from. The following steps will show us how to rapidly change our chart design and get the look and feel you are trying to convey to your audience.

1. Select the chart, click on the **CHART TOOLS** tab, and make sure that the **DESIGN** option is selected.

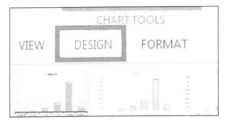

Figure 9.21

2. Click on the **Quick Layout** button, as shown in the following screenshot. Hover over any of the layouts and you will see that your chart is presented in many different ways. This is just another tool Excel gives you to tweak your charts until you get them exactly how you want them to be.

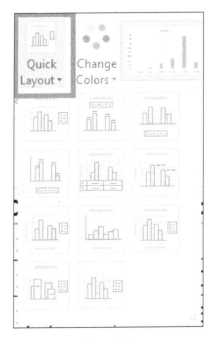

Figure 9.22

Summary

We only touched on the surface of the extensive charting capabilities of Excel. You will now be able to generate charts with just a click of a few buttons to quickly visualize your data. And why do we do this? We do this to get a better feel and understanding of our data. You also saw concrete examples of how to change certain chart elements such as the axis and title. The latter part of the chapter showed you many tools you can use to further customize your charts. From changing the color and the feel all the way to changing the layout. With all of these tools under your belt, visualizing your data should not be intimidating but a joy. The presentation of your data is very important and Excel is your friend at this stage of the data analysis life cycle. The next chapter will expand on this one and give you additional tools to effectively and interactively tell your data stories.

10
Creating Interactive Spreadsheets Using Tables and Slicers

This chapter introduces additional materials to the advanced Excel developer in the presentation stage of the **data analysis life cycle**. In the previous chapter, we learned how to create tables and charts, but in this chapter, we will make them come to life. So far, we have been representing data in a static fashion. What do I mean by representing data in a static way? I mean the Excel report that we have developed so far is not interactive. What you will learn in this chapter is how to leverage Excel's new features to add interactivity to your spreadsheets.

What are slicers?

Slicers are essentially buttons that automatically filter your data. Excel has always been able to filter data, but slicers are more practical and visually appealing. Let's compare the two in the following steps:

1. First, fire up Excel 2013, and create a new spreadsheet. Manually enter the data, as shown in the following screenshot:

Company	Type	MPG	Price	# of Passengers
Toyota	SUV	30	$ 30,000	4
Honda	Sedan	32	$ 45,000	4
Lexus	Sport	21	$ 26,000	6
Hundai	SUV	21	$ 47,000	5
Porshe	Sedan	12	$ 30,000	6
Fiat	Sport	23	$ 40,000	8
Toyota	SUV	21	$ 36,000	4
Honda	Sedan	30	$ 15,000	3
Lexus	Sport	41	$ 67,000	6
Hundai	SUV	30	$ 40,000	4

2. Highlight cells **A1** through **E11**, and press *Ctrl + T* to convert our data into an Excel table. Converting your data into a table is the first step that you need to take in order to introduce slicers in your spreadsheet.

3. Let's filter our data using the default filtering capabilities that we are already familiar with. Filter the **Type** column and only select the rows that have the value equal to **SUV**, as shown in the following screenshot. Click on the **OK** button to apply the filter to the table.

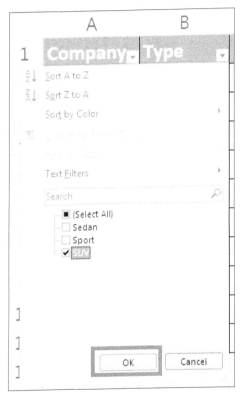

You will now be left with four rows that have the **Type** column equal to **SUV**.

	A	B	C	D	E
1	Company	Type	MPG	Price	# of Passengers
2	Toyota	SUV	30	$ 30,000	4
5	Hundai	SUV	21	$ 47,000	5
8	Toyota	SUV	21	$ 36,000	4
11	Hundai	SUV	30	$ 40,000	4

Using a typical Excel filter, we were able to filter our data and only show all of the SUV cars. We can then continue to filter by other columns, such as **MPG (miles per gallon)** and **Price**. How can we accomplish the same results using slicers? Continue reading this chapter to find this out.

How to create slicers

In this chapter, we will be going through simple but powerful steps that are required to build slicers. After we create our first slicer, make sure that you compare and contrast the old way of filtering with the new way of filtering data.

1. Remove the filter that we just applied to our table by clicking on the option named **Clear Filter From "Type"**, as shown in the following screenshot:

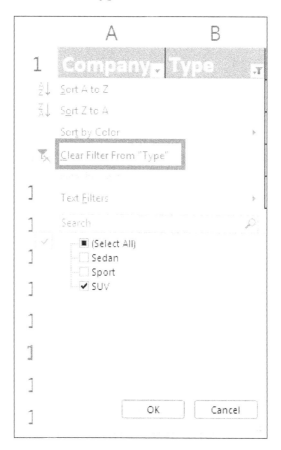

2. With your Excel table selected, click on the **TABLE TOOLS** tab.

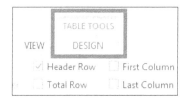

3. Click on the **Insert Slicer** button.

4. In the **Insert Slicers** dialog box, select the **Type** checkbox and click on the **OK** button, as shown in the following screenshot:

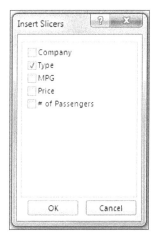

You should now have a slicer that looks similar to the one in the following screenshot. Notice that you can resize and move the slicer anywhere you want in the spreadsheet.

5. Click on the **Sedan** filter in the slicer that we built in the previous step. Wow! The data is filtered and only the rows where the **Type** column is equal to **Sedan** are shown in the results.

6. Click on the **Sport** filter and see what happens. The data is now filtered where the **Type** column is equal to **Sport**. Notice that the previous filter of **Sedan** was removed as soon as we clicked on the **Sport** filter.

7. What if we want to filter the data by both **Sport** and **Sedan**? We can just highlight both the filters with our mouse, or click on **Sedan**, press *Ctrl*, and then, click on the **Sport** filter. The end result will look like this:

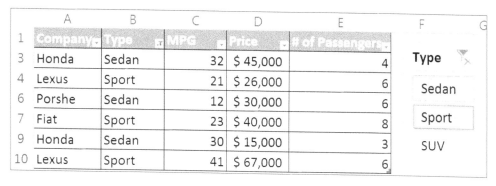

8. To clear the filter, just click on the **Clear Filter** button.

Do you see the advantage of slicers over filters? Yes, of course, they are simply better. Filtering between **Sedan**, **Sport**, or **SUV** is very easy and convenient. It will certainly take less key strokes and the feedback is instant. Think about the end users interacting with your spreadsheet. At the touch of a button, they can answer questions that arise in their heads. This is what you call an interactive spreadsheet or an interactive dashboard.

Styling slicers

There are not many options to style slicers but Excel does give you a decent amount of color schemes that you can experiment with:

1. With the **Type** slicer selected, navigate to the **SLICER TOOLS** tab, as shown in the following screenshot:

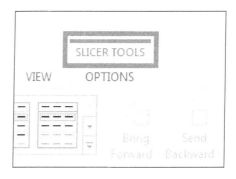

2. Click on the various slicer styles available to get a feel of what Excel offers.

Adding multiple slicers

You are able to add multiple slicers and multiple charts in one spreadsheet. Why would we do this? Well, this is the beginning of a dashboard creation. Let's expand on the example we have just been working on, and see how we can turn raw data into an interactive dashboard:

1. Let's start with creating slicers for **# of Passengers** and **MPG**, as shown in the following screenshot:

2. Rename Sheet1 as **Data**, and create a new sheet called **Dashboard**, as shown here:

3. Move the three slicers by cutting and pasting them from the **Data** sheet to the **Dashboard** sheet.

4. Create a line chart using the columns **Company** and **MPG**, as shown in the following screenshot:

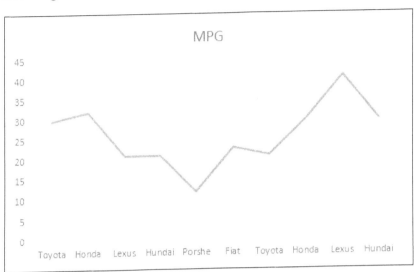

5. Create a bar chart using the columns **Type** and **MPG**.

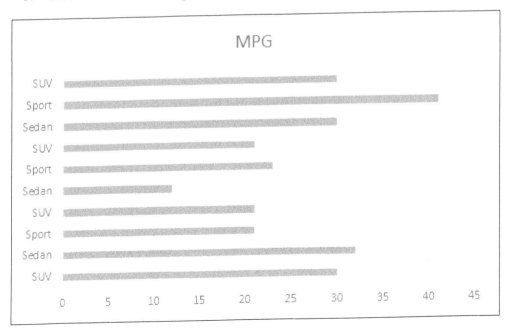

6. Create another bar chart with the columns **company** and **# of Passengers**, as shown in the following screenshot. These types of charts are technically called **column charts,** but you can get away with calling them bar charts.

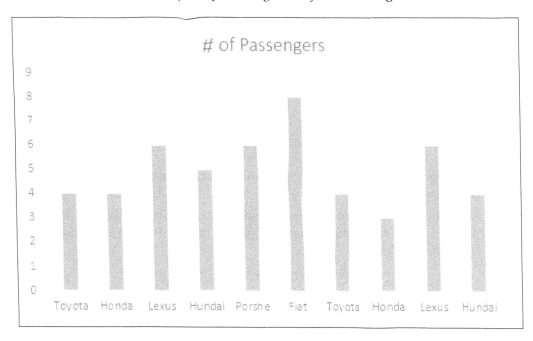

7. Now, move the three charts from the **Data** tab to the **Dashboard** tab. Right-click on the bar chart and select the **Move Chart...** option.

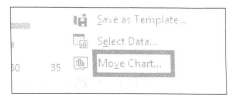

8. In the **Move Chart** dialog box, change the **Object in:** parameter from **Data** to **Dashboard** and then click on the **OK** button.

9. Move the other two charts to the **Dashboard** tab so that there are no more charts in the **Data** tab.

10. Rearrange the charts and slicers so that they resemble as closely as possible the ones in the following screenshot. As you can see this tab is starting to look like a dashboard.

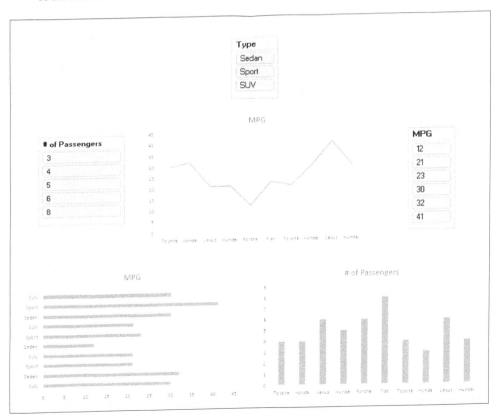

11. The **Type** slicer will look better if **Sedan**, **Sport**, and **SUV** are laid out horizontally. Select the **Type** slicer and click on the **SLICER TOOLS** menu option.

12. Change the **Columns** parameter from 1 to 3, as shown in the following screenshot. This is how we are able to change the layout or shape of the slicer.

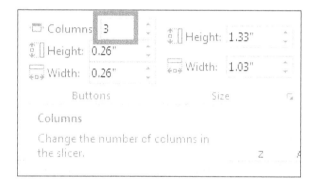

13. Resize the **Type** slicer so that it looks like the one in the following screenshot:

Clearing filters

You can click on one or more filters in the dashboard that we just created. Very cool! Every time we select a filter, all of the three charts that we created get updated. This again is called adding interactivity to your spreadsheets. This allows the end users of your dashboard to interact with your data and perform their own analysis. If you notice, there isn't a good way of removing multiple filters at once. For example, if you select **Sedans** that have a MPG of greater than or equal to 30, how would you remove all of the filters? You would have to clear the filters from the **Type** slicer and then from the **MPG** slicer. This can be a little tedious for your end user, and you will want to avoid this at any cost. The next steps will show you how to create a button using VBA that will filter all of our data in a flash:

1. Press *Alt + F11* and create a sub procedure called `Clear_Slicer`, as shown in the following screenshot. This code will basically find all of the filters that you have selected and then manually clears them for you one at a time. The next step is to bind this code to a button:

```
Sub Clear_Slicer()

    ' Declare Variables
    Dim cache As SlicerCache

    ' Loop through each filter
    For Each cache In ActiveWorkbook.SlicerCaches
        ' clear filter
        cache.ClearManualFilter
    Next cache

End Sub
```

2. Select the **DEVELOPER** tab and click on the **Insert** button. In the pop-up menu called **Form Controls**, select the **Button** option.

3. Now, click anywhere on the sheet, and you will get a dialog box that looks like the following screenshot. This is where we are going to assign a macro to the button. This means that whenever you click on the button we are creating, Excel will run the macro of our choice. Since we have already created a macro called **Clear_Slicer**, it will make sense to select this macro, and then click on the **OK** button.

4. Change the text of the button to **Clear All Filters** and resize it so that it looks like this:

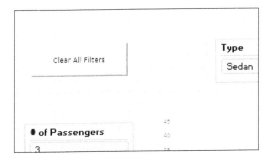

5. Adjust the properties of the button by right-clicking on the button and selecting the **Format Control...** option. Here, you can change the font size and the color of your button label.

6. Now, select a bunch of filters, and click on our new shiny button. Yes, that was pretty cool. The most important part is that it is now even easier to *reset* your dashboard and start a brand new analysis. What do I mean by start a brand new analysis? In general, when a user initially starts using your dashboard, he/she will click on the filters aimlessly. The users do this just to figure out how to mechanically use the dashboard. Then, after they get the hang of it, they want to start with a clean slate and perform some data analysis. If we did not have the **Clear All Filters** button, the users would have to figure out how they would clear every slicer one at a time to start over. The worst case scenario is when the user does not realize when the filters are turned on and when they are turned off. Now, do not laugh at this situation, or assume that your end user is not as smart as you are. This just means that you need to lower the learning curve of your dashboard and make it easy to use. With the addition of the **Clear All Filters** button, the end user can think of a question, use the slicers to answer it, click on the **Clear All Filters** button, and start the process all over again. These little details are what will separate you from the average Excel developer.

Final tweaks

Here is where we start looking at our dashboard and making sure that everything looks okay. Does the data make sense? Can we change some of the charts? These are the types of questions we need to ask ourselves and even our coworkers if possible. You might get ideas or find issues if you just ask someone for their opinion. We are also going to style our charts and slicers to get the feel we are looking for. It is not required that you create a spectacular dashboard, but if you have the time, it is worth the time and effort.

1. I'm not happy with the **MPG** chart. This chart has **SUV** on the *y* axis multiple times, and this can be very confusing for anyone who looks at the dashboard. Let's remove this chart and replace it with a different one. Create a scatter plot with the columns **MPG** and **Price**.

2. Move the new chart to the **Dashboard** tab and delete the old MPG bar chart. Create a border around the charts by inserting a rectangle, as shown in the following screenshot:

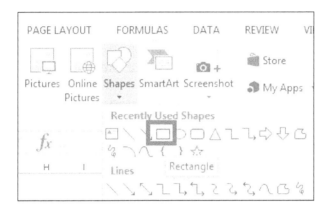

3. Rearrange your charts, slicers, and buttons. Is this the best layout that we can come up with? Certainly not, but you can see that our dashboard is getting closer to our final product. This process forces you to bring out your creative side, and do not worry if you think you don't have a creative side. Over time, you will begin to develop your own style and even enjoy this part of the process.

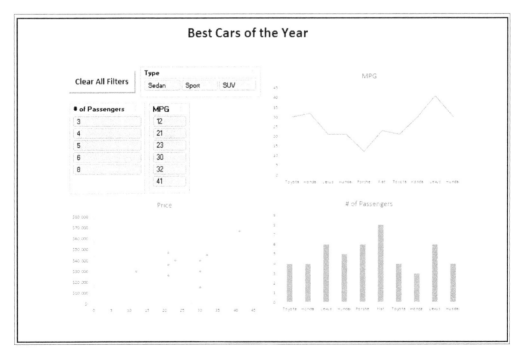

4. Now, let's update the line chart and adjust some of its elements. Change the title to say, Company vs MPG, add the **Miles Per Gallon** label to the *y* axis, and add the **Company** label to the *x* axis, as shown in the following screenshot:

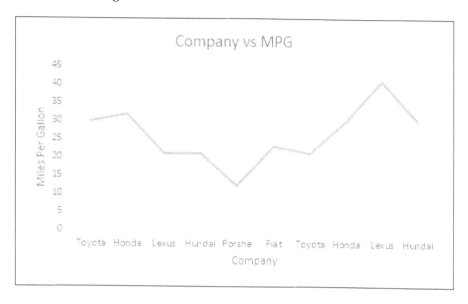

5. Update the scatter chart and adjust some of its elements. Change the title to say, **MPG vs Price**, add the **Miles Per Gallon** label to the *x* axis, and add the **Price** label to the *y* axis.

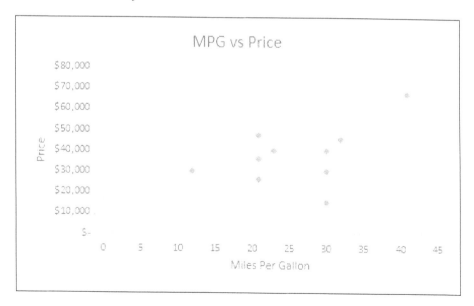

6. Update the bar chart and adjust some of its elements. Change the title to say, **Number of Passengers**, add the **Company** label to the x axis, and add the **# of Passengers** label to the y axis.

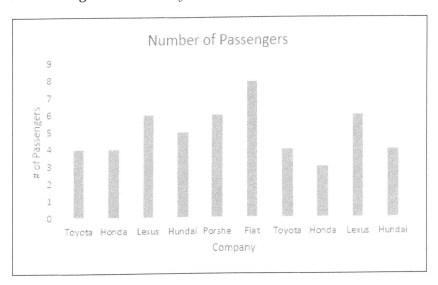

7. Change the slicer styles to match the ones in the following screenshot. You may want to further customize the look of the **Clear All Filters** button, but in this example, we are going to keep the default look.

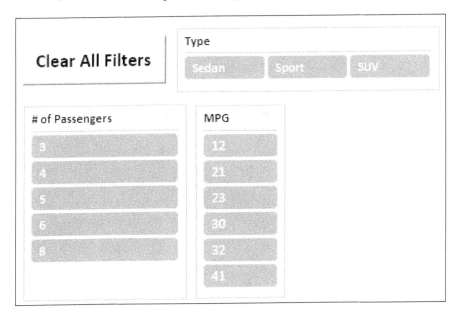

8. By changing the styles of the charts, you will be able to achieve a look that is similar to the following screenshot:

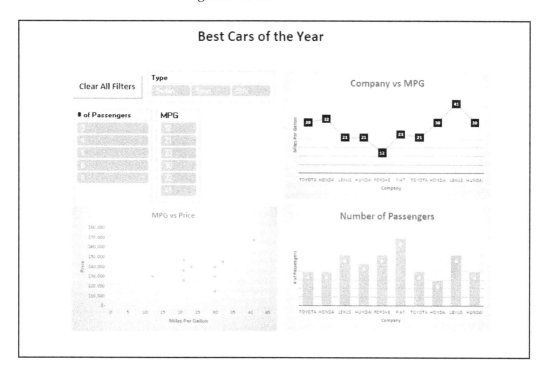

9. For the line chart, I chose **Style 2** but changed the data point label's background to the color black. I did this because the default style made it difficult for me to see the numbers clearly. How do you do this? Right-click on a data point, as shown in the following screenshot:

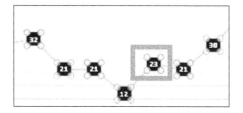

10. In the **Format Data Labels** menu, select the **Fill & Line** menu option, then select **Solid fill**, and change the color to black.

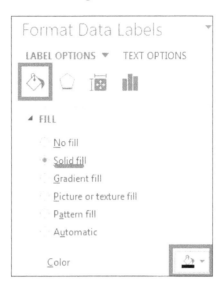

11. The bar chart has the **Style 5** with no additional changes, but unfortunately, there was not a similar style for the scatter chart. This means that I had to try to recreate this style using the **Format Chart Area** option, as shown in the following screenshot. You can just play with the highlighted parameters until you are happy with the results.

Summary

The aim of this chapter was to give you ideas and tools to present your data artistically. Whether you like it or not, sometimes a better-looking analysis will trump the better but less attractive one. Excel gives you the tools to not be on the short end of the stick but to always be able to present visually stunning analysis. You now have your Excel slicers, and you learned how to bind them to your data. Users of your spreadsheet can now slice and dice your data to answer multiple questions. Executives like flashy visualizations, and when you combine them with a strong analysis, you have a very powerful combination. In this chapter, we also went through a variety of strategies to customize slicers and chart elements. These little changes made to your dashboards will make them stand out and help you get your message across. I hope you have enjoyed your journey through the **data analysis life cycle** and now understand all the work that is required to go from raw data to a data story. Excel as always has been an invaluable tool that gives you all of the tools necessary to overcome any data challenges you might come across. As I tell all my students, the key to become better is simply to practice, practice, and practice. The last chapter of the book is a compilation of all of the tips and tricks that we have covered throughout the book. Enjoy!

Tips, Tricks, and Shortcuts

Shortcuts

Shortcut keys	Description
Ctrl + S	This saves a file
Ctrl + C	This copies the selected cells
Ctrl + ; (semicolon)	This enters the current date
Ctrl + V	This inserts the contents of the clipboard at the insertion point
Ctrl + X	This cuts the selected cells
Ctrl + B	This makes the text bold
Ctrl + I	This italicizes the text
Ctrl + 1	This displays the **Format Cells** dialog box
Ctrl + T	This displays the **Create Table** dialog box
Alt + E + S + V	This pastes values only
Alt + E + D	This deletes the selected cells
Shift + Space	This selects the entire row
Ctrl + Space	This selects the entire column
Ctrl + E	The flashes the **Fill** menu
F2	This edits the active cell
Ctrl + A	This selects all the cells
Alt + O + C + A	This resizes the width of the selected cell(s)
Shift + Ctrl + Arrow key	This highlights all the rows with values in the current column
Ctrl + Down arrow key	This goes to the last cell with data

Shortcut keys	Description
Shift + F11	This creates a new sheet
Alt + F11	This opens the VBA Editor
Alt + F8	This opens the **Macro** window
Ctrl + Y	This repeats the last action taken

Tips and tricks

The following are some tips and tricks for your use with Excel:

1. You can also drag the actual `data.txt` file into Excel and this will activate the **Text Import Wizard** (*Chapter 1, Getting Data into Excel*).

2. You can edit cells in the formula bar instead of editing in the actual cell (*Chapter 3, How to Clean Texts, Numbers, and Dates*).

3. You can also double-click on the **+** icon that appears when you hover over the lower-right corner of the cell, and Excel will automatically apply the formula to all of the cells (*Chapter 3, How to Clean Texts, Numbers, and Dates*).

4. Make sure that you make a copy of your original data before you start working on it. This will help you prevent losing any of your original data (*Chapter 3, How to Clean Texts, Numbers, and Dates*).

5. Selecting the entire worksheet before applying a filter to your data is recommended. The advantage is that the same steps can be performed regardless of the number of rows and columns you are working with (*Chapter 3, How to Clean Texts, Numbers, and Dates*).

6. Clicking on the top-left corner of your spreadsheet will select all the columns and rows (*Chapter 3, How to Clean Text, Numbers, and Dates*).

7. You do not need to activate the **DEVELOPER** tab in order to open the VBA Editor. Simply press the *Alt + F11* keys to open the editor (*Chapter 8, Learning VBA – Excel's Scripting Language*).

8. You can learn a lot of VBA code by just recording macros and studying the code that Excel generates for us (*Chapter 8, Learning VBA – Excel's Scripting Language*).

9. You can make your chart title dynamic by adding a formula to the chart title label (*Chapter 9, How to Build and Style Your Charts*).

Index

A

analyzing data 86

B

bar chart (column chart) 163
built-in functions
  using 70-72

C

cells
  capitalizing 48, 49
charting options
  about 167-172
  chart elements 173
  chart filters 174, 175
  chart styles 173
column charts 187
columns
  comparing 75-78
conditional statements 72-75

D

dashboard
  final tweaks 193-198
data
  analyzing 107-110
  combining from multiple columns to one
    column 55-57
  creating manually 4-7
  gathering 79, 80, 101-104
  importing, from CSV file 12
  importing, from sources 7

  importing, from text file 8-12
  importing, from Web 16-19
  preparing 104-106
  preparing, for analysis 80-86
data analysis
  about 86
  applications, processing 86-99
data analysis life cycle
  about 1
  data, analyzing 2
  data, gathering 1
  data, preparing 2
  data, presenting 3
database 24
data models 110-114
domain knowledge 85
duplicate data
  about 49
  identifying 49-52
  removing 49-52

E

Excel files
  importing 13-16
Excel macro 140
Excel Solver
  about 118
  activating 118-120
  using 126-138
extra spaces, in between strings 38-47

F

formulas
  creating 67, 68

H

Hello World VBA script
about 142-144
conditional statements 149, 150
loops 150-152
macro powered spreadsheets, saving 160
macros, creating without code 152-160
variables, declaring 145-149

L

leading spaces 38-47
linear programming 117, 125
linear programming problem
modeling 120-126
line chart (time series chart) 163

M

Microsoft SQL Server database 21
MPG (miles per gallon) 181
MSSQL
Fast forms 21
multiple tables, reading from 26-29
reading from, SQL used 29-35
table, reading from 21-26
users 22

P

pie chart 163

Q

quick analysis charts 164-167

S

scatter chart 164
shortcut keys 201, 202
similar words
fixing 57-62
slicers
about 179-181
creating 181-184
filters, clearing 190-192
multiple slicers, adding 185-189
styling 184
strings
and numbers, combining 69, 70
Structured Query Language (SQL) 21

T

text to columns 52-54
text to dates 62, 63
text to numbers 64, 65
tips and tricks 202
trailing spaces 38-47

V

VBA (Visual Basic for Applications) 139
VBA Editor
about 140
opening 140-142
VLOOKUP function 104

Thank you for buying
Data Analysis and Business Modeling
with Excel 2013

About Packt Publishing

Packt, pronounced 'packed', published its first book, *Mastering phpMyAdmin for Effective MySQL Management*, in April 2004, and subsequently continued to specialize in publishing highly focused books on specific technologies and solutions.

Our books and publications share the experiences of your fellow IT professionals in adapting and customizing today's systems, applications, and frameworks. Our solution-based books give you the knowledge and power to customize the software and technologies you're using to get the job done. Packt books are more specific and less general than the IT books you have seen in the past. Our unique business model allows us to bring you more focused information, giving you more of what you need to know, and less of what you don't.

Packt is a modern yet unique publishing company that focuses on producing quality, cutting-edge books for communities of developers, administrators, and newbies alike. For more information, please visit our website at www.packtpub.com.

About Packt Enterprise

In 2010, Packt launched two new brands, Packt Enterprise and Packt Open Source, in order to continue its focus on specialization. This book is part of the Packt Enterprise brand, home to books published on enterprise software – software created by major vendors, including (but not limited to) IBM, Microsoft, and Oracle, often for use in other corporations. Its titles will offer information relevant to a range of users of this software, including administrators, developers, architects, and end users.

Writing for Packt

We welcome all inquiries from people who are interested in authoring. Book proposals should be sent to author@packtpub.com. If your book idea is still at an early stage and you would like to discuss it first before writing a formal book proposal, then please contact us; one of our commissioning editors will get in touch with you.

We're not just looking for published authors; if you have strong technical skills but no writing experience, our experienced editors can help you develop a writing career, or simply get some additional reward for your expertise.

Practical Data Science Cookbook

ISBN: 978-1-78398-024-6   Paperback: 396 pages

89 hands-on recipes to help you complete real-world data science projects in R and Python

1. Learn about the data science pipeline and use it to acquire, clean, analyze, and visualize data.

2. Understand critical concepts in data science in the context of multiple projects.

3. Expand your numerical programming skills through step-by-step code examples and learn more about the robust features of R and Python.

Practical Data Analysis

ISBN: 978-1-78328-099-5   Paperback: 360 pages

Transform, model, and visualize your data through hands-on projects, developed in open source tools

1. Explore how to analyze your data in various innovative ways and turn them into insight.

2. Learn to use the D3.js visualization tool for exploratory data analysis.

3. Understand how to work with graphs and social data analysis.

4. Discover how to perform advanced query techniques and run MapReduce on MongoDB.

Please check **www.PacktPub.com** for information on our titles

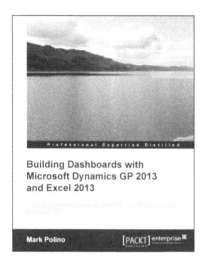

Building Dashboards with Microsoft Dynamics GP 2013 and Excel 2013

ISBN: 978-1-84968-906-9   Paperback: 268 pages

Easily build powerful dashboards with Microsoft Dynamics GP 2013 and Excel 2013

1. Build a dashboard using Excel 2013 with information from Microsoft Dynamics GP 2013.

2. Make Excel a true business intelligence tool with charts, sparklines, slicers, and more.

3. Utilize PowerPivot's full potential to create even more complex dashboards.

Excel Programming with VBA Starter

ISBN: 978-1-84968-844-4   Paperback: 60 pages

Get started with programming in Excel using Visual Basic for Applications (VBA)

1. Learn something new in an Instant! A short, fast, focused guide delivering immediate results.

2. Extend and enhance your Excel spreadsheets using the power of Macros and VBA programming.

3. Get to grips with the VBA language to create professional spreadsheets.